Praise for *This Book Will Make You Kinder*

'Henry is a master at softening hearts and making people understand and care – his work encourages us to regularly put ourselves in other people's shoes. *This Book Will Make You Kinder* is not just beautiful to look at but feels urgent in its message. For many reasons we are in danger of becoming disconnected and dehumanised, and this book is a reminder of the life-changing power of empathy. I hope this book makes it into every school and onto every bookshelf' Emma Gannon

'Blends distinctly human comics with an academic approach to understanding empathy, from a near-expert on the subject. The result is an affirming, charming book that ultimately lives up to its title' Adam J. Kurtz

'If kindness and empathy is the best of humanity this book is a roadmap to it. Accessible, beautifully illustrated, at times heart-swelling in its wholesomeness and at others inviting you to consider philosophical ideas, it'll sink your brain into a warm bath and, in turn, you'll return a kinder person ready to raise the bar on humanity' Gina Martin

'Interspersed with Henry's beautifully metaphorical illustrations, this is a great and easy-reading practical exploration of what kindness means in the modern world' Matt Haig

'Foundational to our humanity, crucial to our survival, and only limited by our imagination and will, this book will convince you to take a hard look at the "mistakes" that hamper your capacity for kindness, the power structures that depend on those limitations and the moral imperative we all have to overcome them. Both a compelling philosophical exploration of morality and a strategic guide to expanding our collective capacity for empathy, this slim book makes an elegant (and beautifully illustrated) case for power of kindness. Smart, huma   McBee

This Book
Will Make You
Kinder

An Empathy Handbook

HENRY JAMES GARRETT

SOUVENIR
PRESS

This paperback edition first published in 2021

First published in Great Britain in 2020 by
Souvenir Press,
an imprint of Profile Books Ltd
29 Cloth Fair
London
EC1A 7JQ
www.souvenirpress.com

First published in the United States in 2020 by
Penguin Books, an imprint of Penguin Random House

Designed by Sabrina Bowers

1 3 5 7 9 10 8 6 4 2

Printed in Great Britain by Bell & Bain Ltd., Glasgow

The moral right of the author has been asserted.

A CIP catalogue record for this book is available from the British Library.

ISBN 978 1 78816 549 5
eISBN 978 1 78283 720 6
Audio ISBN 978 1 78283 792 3

For my parents, who gave all that they are to make me all that I am.
And for Kitty. Some worry that being too sensitive to the suffering of others
forces one to withdraw from doing the work; to them I would like to
introduce Kitty, the softest soul and yet the most relentless kindness warrior,
who does the work every fucking day.

•••• Contents ••••

This is a book about kindness as well as its absence and opposite. For that reason, it includes examples of cruelties no one should experience, which many people do. Violence, trauma, and oppression alter the mind-body in ways that those of us privileged enough to have avoided such experiences are rarely cognizant of. An unexpected reference that calls forth a memory or triggers something bodily in someone who has survived what they should never have experienced can cause intolerable suffering. Requests for content notes, then, are not cases of people being oversensitive—that belief is born of a failure of empathy (more on that to come). All this to say: Content notes are necessary, not a big ask, and this is one.

This book will make reference to: sexual violence, rape, dehumanization, mental illness, classism, poverty, migrantism, border policing, homelessness, fatphobia, transphobia, colonialism, police violence, ableism, interphobia, racism, sexism, homophobia, animal cruelty, and dogs attacking a human.

•••• Introduction ••••

This book will make you kinder. I'm not picking on you;
it's just that you're the one reading it. This book will
hopefully make anyone who reads it kinder and will hopefully
be read by loads of people.

I've found that I have to write a book that makes people
kinder.

The reason I have to do that has something to do with the
fact that I suffer from anxiety. Anxiety sufferers vary a lot;
what triggers paralyzing fear in one can be very different from
what terrifies another. Some people are stressed by large, open
spaces; others, by confined ones; some unfortunate people are
stressed by both.

One of the many things that I find anxiety-inducing is unkindness, including my own. My whole body seizes up in panic
when I notice the most minor inadvertent hurts people cause
one another. You can imagine the stress that a populist back-
lash against basic forms of human decency is causing me.

I want the world to be less cruel so that I can find it a less
stressful place to live (an ironically selfish motive for creating a
better world).

But thanks to the aforementioned anxiety, I'm terrified by many of the routes I might take to make the world kinder. Most of the ways one could go about changing things involve meeting people and talking with them face-to-face. And, stressful though unkindness is, I find interacting with strangers even more so.

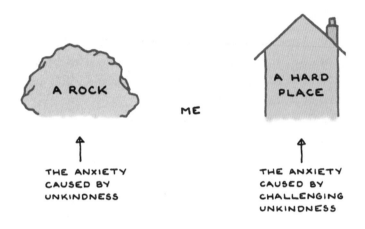

A ROCK

ME

A HARD PLACE

THE ANXIETY CAUSED BY UNKINDNESS

THE ANXIETY CAUSED BY CHALLENGING UNKINDNESS

I'm caught between a rock and a terrifying social situation: desperate to make people kinder, but stressed out by actually having to talk to them about it.

So a book seems the best route forward for me. If I can sit here, on my own, in my slippers, and write something that will drastically increase your kindness—without us ever having to actually meet—that's the dream scenario for me.

This is that book.

This Book
Will Make
You Kinder

AN EMPATHY HANDBOOK

Henry James Garrett

(Secretly, I'm hoping that billions of people read this book and that they all suddenly become as kind as the kindest person I know. Then I can sneak off and live in a tree house with my partner and feel like I did my bit. I don't think it's particularly likely, but it's worth a shot.)

There's one thing I need you to know from the start: I'm not writing this book because I think I'm particularly kind. I don't. I'm not writing from a place of kindness superiority. I've just spent a lot of time thinking about kindness and its limits, because I spend so much of my time stressed out by all the cruelty. And I was lucky enough to get a chance to write those thoughts down.

In fact, this book represents my second attempt to write down these very musings. The first was a few years ago. I had thought for some reason that the best place to go to write stuff that would make people kinder was an academic philosophy department.

So, I started a philosophy PhD (on the subject of empathy and metaethics). My goal was to become a professor who wrote papers so compelling that they left the academic sphere and convinced everyone to be more moral. Instead, it was I who left academia. My anxiety (compounded, perhaps, by those unrealistic aspirations) forced me to drop out of my studies.

At that point, I began working in earnest on these drawings. I needed a way to feel I was contributing to a kinder world, as well as a job that my anxiety would allow me to do, and I was spending most of my time with my dog, Billie, who's always cared for me when I've been unwell. Hence, Drawings of Dogs—and my peculiar cartooning career—was born (I've since branched out from just drawing dogs).

I draw anthropomorphized animals, plants, and inanimate objects chatting verbosely and try to make gentle, Trojan-horse points about how humans mistreat one another.

I feel ecstatic and incredibly grateful that things have somehow come a weird full circle. Those cartoons (and the generous, beautifully loyal people who've connected with them) have led me here, to writing this book. And what I'm trying to write is a jargon-free version of what I intended to write as a philosopher (with the benefit of everything I've learned in the intervening years as well as a much wider audience): an illustrated book that makes its reader kinder.

YOU + THIS BOOK

=

YOU, BUT KINDER

When I talk about making you kinder, I don't just mean the everyday kindness of taking out your neighbor's bins—although I'd hate to downplay the importance of small acts. I also mean the strong, courageous, moral kindness of fighting injustice or sacrificing something for a worthy cause; I mean the hard work of self-reflection and self-improvement that is the only path to challenging the ways we've been conditioned

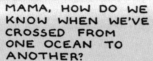

by our society to be cruel to certain groups en masse. I plan to make you kinder in this sense; I mean to cover all the good and bad that we do to one another (I did say it was an unrealistically ambitious book).

In talking about kindness, I'm also talking about all of morality. And you'll notice that I flit back and forth, using those words nearly synonymously. That's because in my view, morality is the domain of thought in which we inquire as to which kindnesses and abstentions from cruelty we owe to and can expect from one another. (The language of morality is often used more broadly than this. People use *immoral* to capture a wide range of prohibitions on behaviors that they find yucky, threatening, or distasteful. But that's not what morality, as I believe it should be understood, is about.)

MORALITY ≠ WHAT I FIND YUCKY

In my view, to say that something is *morally right* is just to say that it's a form of kindness that is required of you. To describe something as *morally wrong* is to say that it's a form of cruelty you mustn't commit.

So, along with making you kinder, this book's going to help you get a firm handle on that most slippery of subjects: morality.[1]

A book that could make everyone kinder, in this sense, is desperately needed right now (although, it's doubtful there's ever been a time it hasn't). Unkindness has been given new energy and legitimacy in recent years. Long-brewing fear and resentment have been redirected from the powerful toward the most powerless people in our society. Cruelty has stepped from the shadows, has rebranded, and now occupies many of the world's highest political offices.

So, how could a book possibly make you kinder? My strategy will be to answer two questions:

OOOOOH, TOPICAL!

- Why are we kind?

- Why aren't we kinder?

Working out why humans are kind at all is a good place to start. If we can't agree on why humans are a bit kind, we're unlikely to agree on the best route to making them all a bit kinder. And I don't think we do agree on the basic source of human kindness.

There are a number of explanations on offer, and they suggest different acceptable limits to our kindness and different routes to expanding those limits. I'll present a specific account of human kindness and morality, one that gives empathy a central role,[2] and build from there in getting us all to step it up a gear.

ONE EXPLANATION
OF HUMAN KINDNESS

MAKING PEOPLE
KINDER

A DIFFERENT
EXPLANATION OF
HUMAN KINDNESS

(A quick aside: I want it to be clear that what I offer here is one account among many of the foundations of morality. Many people will disagree with it, and that's OK. Although I sincerely believe this account to be in some sense *the truth* about morality, and I'd quite like you to agree, I also recognize that other people believe alternative accounts just as sincerely, that I don't have privileged access to the truth of the matter, and that one group trying to enforce its view of morality on another is morally reprehensible—and has, ironically, been the pretext for many atrocities. All of this should go without saying, but it's the fault of people who have tended to look like me that it does not.)

I want to engage you in these abstract questions because it's my view that this is where our moral discrepancies get their foothold, though we tend not to notice it. Arguments about politics, morality, and how we should live rarely end in anyone changing their mind. How often have you felt you're wasting your time in an ethical dispute, like you're a pair of monolingual UN diplomats and all the translators are on strike, leaving you ardently talking past one another in different languages?

People talk past each other on moral matters because their true disagreement exists elsewhere; the real source of disagreement is often that those involved arrived with different ideas about what and how much we owe to one another. When one person's starting point is a far more limited conception of what morality can demand than the other's, there's little chance of them seeing eye-to-eye on specific moral questions. But we never move the conversation further back, to the abstract questions about what morality demands—or what morality even is.

UNDER THE MORALITY
THAT I ACCEPT,
YOU'RE IMMORAL!

UNDER THE MORALITY
THAT I ACCEPT,
YOU'RE IMMORAL!

SHALL WE TALK
ABOUT OUR MORAL
SYSTEMS HEAD-ON?

THAT'S A GREAT
IDEA.

Those who hold narrow views of our duties to one another are wrong, in my view. Those who think, for example, that as long as you're not breaking the law, you can't be acting immorally simply don't get morality.

We owe each other far more than we tend to recognize. But we need to have that conversation head-on. My hope is that when we do, we'll see that we are far from doing enough. This book will help everyone who reads it reset their threshold for how much kindness is owed, leaving you with the realization that we've all been falling short for some time (that's OK, though; it's what we do with that realization that matters).

Most of the books that aim to make you kinder do so by getting specific. They get down to the nitty-gritty in a particular area of politics, applied ethics, or social justice; they try to show you specifically what you've been getting wrong, and how you ought to change your actions going forward. We need books like that; I've read some incredible ones and have had my behavior changed by them.[3]

But with this book, I'm aiming to get a bit more meta. I want to go beyond the specifics, further back than any *particular* kindness question, and see if we can find some solid ground. I want us to move closer to a world in which we arrive at political disputes with a shared background assumption that we owe one another an awful lot, so that we can focus on the problem of how to act on that assumption.

With this book, I'm going to argue that you are kind because of empathy,[4] and the only reason you aren't kinder is because you make mistakes that switch that empathy off.

WHY ARE YOU KIND?

THROUGH EMPATHY, YOU SHARE IN THE FEELINGS OF OTHERS.

WHY AREN'T YOU KINDER?

YOUR EMPATHY IS LIMITED BY MISTAKES.

Our evolved capacity for empathy—our capacity to experience those feelings we witness in others—is in my view (and hopefully in yours, by the end of this book) the source of human kindness and the foundation of morality.

Our automatic tendency to empathetically partake in the pain and pleasure of others is a sufficient explanation of our concern for people's well-being and our motivation to act kindly. But if the empathy you experience right now were the beginning and end of the kindness discussion, there wouldn't be much point in this book.

Turns out, our empathy malfunctions when we make certain types of mistakes.

When you don't know enough about others and how your choices affect them, or when you hold false beliefs that similarly obscure the lived consequences of your actions, it's impossible for your empathy to motivate you to act as it otherwise would. Certain kinds of ignorance can result in you witnessing someone in pain and feeling no part of that pain. Ignorance can switch your empathy off.

Therefore, it's not your actual, currently occurring empathy that counts; it's the empathy you would feel if you weren't making any mistakes. It's empathy in the absence of empathy-limiting ignorance that matters, morally speaking.

Empathy – ignorance = morality (or, the kindness we owe one another).

Making someone kinder, then, has more to do with getting rid of the bad reasons they have for limiting their kindness than it does with providing new reasons to be kind. Ultimately this book is about helping you become better at spotting empathy-limiting mistakes and less prone to making new ones; to that end we'll explore a taxonomy of common types of mistakes.

We must also be mindful of the fact that the ignorance that makes humans cruel is not evenly distributed. And that's because power is not evenly distributed. A large chunk of empathy-limiting mistakes have as their subject members of an oppressed group or marginalized community. It's more likely that people (like me) from more privileged groups will hold those beliefs and maintain that ignorance, which enables us to be cruel to oppressed folk, than vice versa.

Not everyone is equally responsible for the "empathy deficit,"[5]

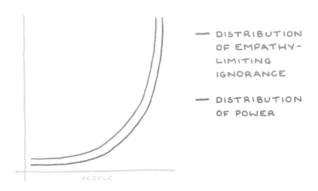

— DISTRIBUTION OF EMPATHY-LIMITING IGNORANCE

— DISTRIBUTION OF POWER

PEOPLE

and I'm at pains to make sure that no one finishes this book thinking that was my message. I'm not claiming that everyone needs to strengthen their empathy toward everyone else; that, for example, survivors of men's sexual violence need to find a way to empathize more wholly with violent men. Not in the slightest.

Oppressed people are already doing a good enough job of empathizing with their oppressors.[6] Our society is set up to encourage only *some* forms of empathy-limiting ignorance: those that justify and therefore cement power. It's set up that way not through some mysterious conspiracy but because only certain types of stories get told; we learn a lot about some groups' experiences and are encouraged in our ignorance of others'.

It follows that the best defense against some of the most common empathy-limiting mistakes is listening to marginalized people directly. If you seek out those voices that have been actively silenced and listen to and believe what they have to say, you'll be far less likely to make a mistake that stops you from empathizing. To be clear, by listening, I don't just mean partaking in audible conversation (in the sense used here, deaf people are able to listen); by listening, I mean an active effort to receive what someone is communicating, through any medium, to you.

TRANSPHOBIA

I don't want you to think that this book is exclusively about political forms of cruelty; the same principles apply in our personal relationships (the dichotomy between personal and political is flawed, but I hope you can see the contrast I'm getting at). In our personal lives we make empathy-limiting mistakes that are uniquely our own. This book will hopefully help us to spot and unmake those too. But when we're talking about those mistakes that are widely shared, we will tend inevitably to be talking about power and identity.

This book will make you kinder in two main ways: It will give you a firm understanding of the foundation of your kindness, which will legitimize and strengthen your moral resolve; and it will provide some tools and a framework to spot those mistakes that limit your empathy and thereby your kindness.

You are kind because of empathy, but your empathy has been unduly limited. I'm hoping to convince you that you owe others at least that kindness you would extend to them if you had talked with them, listening to and believing what they had to say, and were fully aware of their lived experience and how your actions might affect them.

You ought to be as kind as you would be if you knew vividly about every sentient being's life and how you might help—or harm—them. And that would be very kind indeed.

We all already have the capacity for a radically inclusive and demanding form of empathy. My hope is that if we look head-on at what holds us back, the walls around our kindness will crumble.

Why ask,
"Why are we kind?"

Abstract questions

To make people kinder, I'm setting out to answer these two questions:

- Why are we kind?

- Why aren't we kinder?

At this point, I fear you might be thinking this all sounds a little too abstract. Perhaps you're looking around at the volume of socially condoned cruelty in our society and thinking now's not the time for philosophizing. Aren't these theoretical questions just intellectual curiosities, inappropriate in a time when what we really need are practical actions we can take to resist a rising tide of violence?

I THINK, THEREFORE I AM.

THAT'S GREAT, RENÉ, BUT
THE PLANET'S ON FIRE.

I want to convince you that the most abstract moral questions and our answers to them matter.

Usually when we disagree on some isolated moral question—when we can't decide what the kind thing to do is or whether a certain act of kindness is required of us—we conduct our argument on a superficial level.

Let's say you're arguing with one of your friends because you disagree on what your duties are when someone who is street-homeless asks for money to buy a hot drink. One of you might suggest that the money will be put to better use if donated to a homeless shelter, while the other might point out that one of the many dehumanizing aspects of being street-homeless is that everyone you meet thinks they're better placed than you to decide what's in your best interest. Maybe there's also a third friend who says that, though it would be generous to use your money in either of these ways, ultimately it's your hard-earned money and you have no duty whatsoever to do anything about homelessness with it (we're not a fan of this guy).

It's unlikely, I think, that you'd move the argument further back and look for a more abstract origin for your disagreement. Perhaps if you did, you'd find that you have different

takes on what justifies the existence and maintenance of private property rights. Maybe one friend believes those rights are built into the fabric of the universe and the other thinks they're an essential legal construct for a functioning economy, while you recognize these rights as contingent features of our current economic system that allow the wealthy to exploit others. And perhaps it's here that the divergence in your views really lies.

This is a problem that crops up a lot. In fact, it's everywhere I look. People are arguing about the particular, trying to shape one another's views on specific issues, without checking if there's any agreement on the premises they brought to these conversations. However you want to cut it—left versus right, social justice warrior versus fascist, snowflake versus realist— our views on particular, substantive moral questions seem to be decided before we even arrive at those questions.

You can probably bring to mind many of your acquaintances and accurately predict where they will stand on moral issues about which you've never conversed. That's because our views on the right thing to do are determined higher up, or further back. Those views follow from the stances we have implicitly adopted on more abstract moral questions (such as "What sorts of beings are worthy of moral consideration?"), which in turn follow from answers to even more abstract questions (such as "What do we even mean by 'moral'?").

Imagine a group of friends playing a board game. One of them rolls the dice, gets a six, and goes to move their piece, but an argument breaks out over where it should now be. One person thinks it should move six places forward; another, that it should move twenty places back.

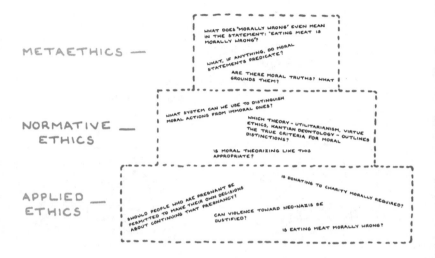

HIERARCHICAL ABSTRACTION OF MORAL QUESTIONS

METAETHICS —

WHAT DOES "MORALLY WRONG" EVEN MEAN IN THE STATEMENT: "EATING MEAT IS MORALLY WRONG"?

WHAT, IF ANYTHING, DO MORAL STATEMENTS PREDICATE?

ARE THERE MORAL TRUTHS? WHAT GROUNDS THEM?

NORMATIVE ETHICS —

WHAT SYSTEM CAN WE USE TO DISTINGUISH MORAL ACTIONS FROM IMMORAL ONES?

WHICH THEORY – UTILITARIANISM, VIRTUE ETHICS, KANTIAN DEONTOLOGY – OUTLINES THE TRUE CRITERIA FOR MORAL DISTINCTIONS?

IS MORAL THEORIZING LIKE THIS APPROPRIATE?

APPLIED ETHICS —

IS DONATING TO CHARITY MORALLY REQUIRED?

SHOULD PEOPLE WHO ARE PREGNANT BE PERMITTED TO MAKE THEIR OWN DECISIONS ABOUT CONTINUING THAT PREGNANCY?

CAN VIOLENCE TOWARD NEO-NAZIS BE JUSTIFIED?

IS EATING MEAT MORALLY WRONG?

Like all the board games of my youth, this imaginary one descends into angry name-calling. But no one asks, "What board game are we even playing?" Had they done so, the group would have quickly re-alized that while one person thought they were playing Monopoly, another thought they were playing Chutes and Ladders.

JUST FOLLOWING ORDERS

No one asked the question that pushed the argument further back, to where the real source of their disagreement lay.

In the case of our moral disagreements, the same thing is happening. We're trying to have very specific arguments about whether such and such is morally bad without ever seeing if we agree on what "morally bad" means.

We don't all agree on what the fundamental source of our kindness is. And that's a conversation we need to have.

Practical consequences

It might be tempting to think that as long as someone behaves kindly, it doesn't really matter how they explain that kindness. I disagree; how we explain kindness has practical consequences. Different explanations suggest different limits to kindness and different routes to making people kinder. Just as vital, without a good explanation of the source of kindness, you've got no answer to give people who doubt it even exists.

HELLO
MY NAME IS
Henry. Please talk to me about moral philosophy (or let me go home, parties make me somewhat anxious).

So, what are the explanations on offer?

If you ask, "Why are people kind?" (that's right, I'm a hoot at parties) these are the responses you tend to get:

"People are kind because we've internalized rules, such as: Don't take what doesn't belong to you; don't pull your sister's hair."

"We're kind because God made us kind."

"It's sometimes rational to be kind. When people are kind, they are simply behaving as rationality demands."

"Humans aren't kind. Sometimes the free market will direct selfishness toward mutually beneficial outcomes, but we're always selfish at root, and don't you forget it."[1]

Try it yourself, maybe. See if this list captures most of the answers you get.

I believe these answers are incorrect. They're not the right account of why humans are kind. And being wrong about the very fundamentals of kindness is a big problem. Each answer paints a different picture of morality and its limits.

For instance, people who believe that kindness exists only thanks to rules and the threat of punishment for breaking them are stuck with a dim view of humanity, in which kindness is born out of fear. They also can never expect kindness to go beyond that which the rules demand.

Have you ever tried to get someone to be a bit kinder, only to have them respond with something like: "Why should I? I'm not breaking any rules!" It's an exasperating response, especially when used to defend real cruelty. But if rules explain kindness, it makes sense.

The true explanation of human kindness is needed now perhaps more than ever. It's vital in unkind times that people believe in kindness, that we all have some confidence in the

KINDNESS EXPLANATIONS AND KINDNESS LIMITS

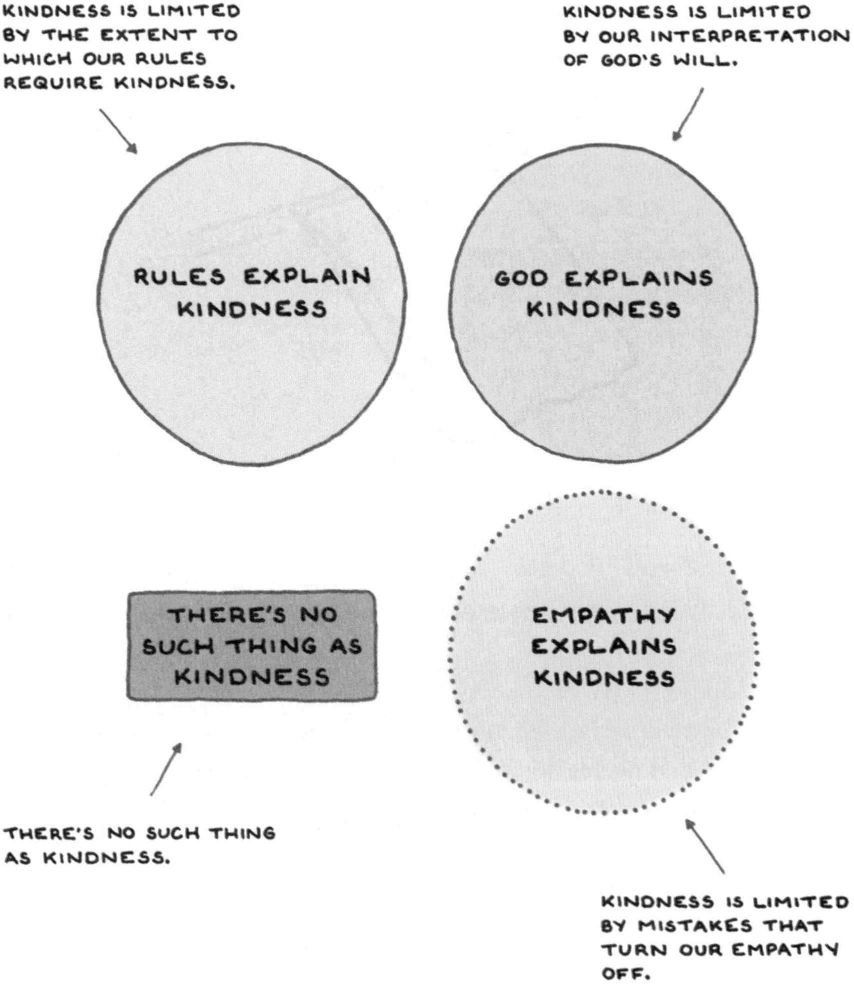

KINDNESS IS LIMITED
BY THE EXTENT TO
WHICH OUR RULES
REQUIRE KINDNESS.

KINDNESS IS LIMITED
BY OUR INTERPRETATION
OF GOD'S WILL.

RULES EXPLAIN
KINDNESS

GOD EXPLAINS
KINDNESS

THERE'S NO
SUCH THING AS
KINDNESS

EMPATHY
EXPLAINS
KINDNESS

THERE'S NO SUCH THING
AS KINDNESS.

KINDNESS IS LIMITED
BY MISTAKES THAT
TURN OUR EMPATHY
OFF.

foundations of morality. We need to be able to point to the kindness source, so that we can say: Actually, kindness isn't optional. It isn't some side effect of market forces; it isn't a softness produced by the coddling of snowflake millennials. Kindness is built into the fabric of what it is to be human, and once we understand that, we'll realize just how much kinder we could—and should—be.

HUMAN FABRIC
5% SELF-INTEREST
5% KINDNESS
90% WORRYING THAT EVERYONE BUT YOU KNOWS WHAT THEY'RE DOING
MADE IN AFRICA

We (might) owe each other so much more

Before we move on, one more little aside. I worry that one of the barriers we face when we talk about how much kindness we owe is that people don't want to accidentally arrive at the conclusion that we owe one another much, much more.

It's a barrier that often crops up when someone tries to introduce a demanding account of our moral duties; people see it coming and stop listening. Because, of course, few of us want to think of ourselves as having been falling morally short for

some time, and few of us want to acknowledge the hard work required to rectify that shortcoming.

A specific fallacy is crucial in creating this mental block to more demanding accounts of what we owe one another. We tend not to state it explicitly, but it serves as a comforting, implicit pattern of thought that helps us avoid demands for greater kindness. It takes roughly the following form:

> If, "x is morally required" is true, then I (and many people I respect) have been failing to do what is morally required.

> Therefore, "x is morally required" is false.

This fallacy has done more harm than most. It allows us to use our current model of our moral duties as a sort of benchmark and to mistakenly conclude that it's impossible that we are very far from doing what is right.

The missing premise of this position is: "It cannot be the case that I (and many people I respect) have been failing to do what is morally required." But if millennia of human history have taught us anything, it's that we can't rely on that being true. It is distinctly possible that you and I and all the people we know are getting things wrong from the moral perspective, just as many of our ancestors have done. It is distinctly possible—and I'd say highly likely—that most of us are currently failing to recognize or act on requirements to be much kinder.

In this book, we'll arrive at an account of why we are kind—and why we aren't kinder—that suggests that there's probably a whole lot of room for you to do a whole lot more. We have a shared idea of where "kind enough" lies, but I'll claim that it's

KINDNESS SCALE

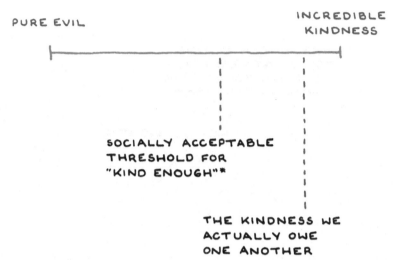

PURE EVIL

INCREDIBLE KINDNESS

SOCIALLY ACCEPTABLE THRESHOLD FOR "KIND ENOUGH"*

THE KINDNESS WE ACTUALLY OWE ONE ANOTHER

* THIS THRESHOLD, LIKE MOST SOCIAL NORMS, VARIES WITH IDENTITY FACTORS LIKE RACE AND GENDER.

not nearly kind enough. And I'm going to ask that you try not to shut down.

I want you to read the rest of this book (and, if at all possible, live the rest of your life) with a view to the possibility that we owe each other so, so much more.

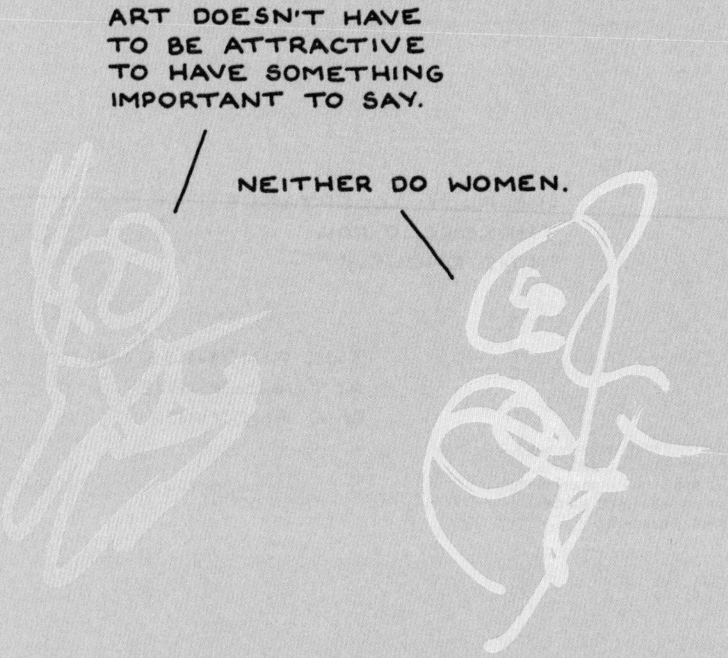

ART DOESN'T HAVE
TO BE ATTRACTIVE
TO HAVE SOMETHING
IMPORTANT TO SAY.

NEITHER DO WOMEN.

●●●● 2 ●●●●

We are kind
because of empathy

Why are we kind?

So, why are we kind? We are kind (to the extent we are) because we possess the capacity for empathy.[1]

This is a simple answer. But it's an answer that explains how kindness feels on an emotional level, that doesn't repaint kindness as selfishness in disguise, and that doesn't set hard limits on our kindness, but instead points the way to a dramatic expansion. However, it's not an answer that everyone agrees on.

Empathy is a superpower. Being empathetic is a bit like being telepathic, but rather than walking around overhearing other people's internal dialogue, you automatically take on a shadow of their experiential state. We don't even need to control it; it just happens. It's probably not a sufficiently dramatic power to guarantee entry to the Avengers, but it's essential, I believe, in the development of morality.

Empathy is the ability we have to notice someone in pain and to feel some part of that pain. And it doesn't just work for pain; it works for joy, sadness, anger, pleasure, hunger, stress, and a hundred other feelings that we might not even have words for. If you can feel it, you can feel it empathetically too.

OBSERVE SOMEONE FEELING A FEELING

EMPATHY

FEEL SOME SHADOW OF WHAT THEY'RE FEELING

$\left(\begin{array}{c}\text{RECOGNIZE THE OTHER AS THE}\\\text{ORIGIN OF SAID FEELING}\end{array}\right)$

FEEL SOME MOTIVATION TO MAKE THEM FEEL BETTER

ACT KINDLY TOWARD THEM

If you take away one thing from this book (I hope you take away more than one thing, of course), let it be this: We don't need gods, laws, or markets to be moral. People without gods, in lawless societies, are still people with the capacity for empathy. Sharing in each other's pain, sorrow, and joy will always be enough to make people a bit kind to one another. Automatically partaking in every feeling you encounter gives you some motivation to make sure other people are doing OK, and to fight to bring an end to their suffering.

We don't even have to directly observe people's feelings to be motivated to act kindly. We're able to picture the feelings of people who aren't around and to empathize with those feelings. We're also able to imagine the consequences of actions not yet taken, and we can be motivated in our choices by the imagined feelings of the people those actions will affect.

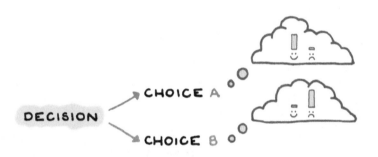

And we can be motivated by empathy even when we don't actually empathize. Sometimes we act out of habit without really sharing in feelings at all; we just know how we would act if we paid attention and empathized, and we get on with acting that way without doing the exercise in feeling. It's not like I picture someone stepping in my dog's poop every time I clean up after her; but I do clean up after her because I know if I did picture that, and empathized with the day it would ruin, that's what I'd end up doing.

Even when we don't go through the process of empathetically partaking in what will be felt as a result of our actions, we can still do the right thing, because we know how we'd feel if we did empathize.

It's thanks to empathy that you care about experiences that are not your own. And that is why you are kind.

Why empathy?

But why empathy? Why do I think this is the best explanation of our kindness?

Remember, there are a number of alternative explanations of kindness on offer. It would be dishonest not to mention that most philosophers subscribe to something like one of those other accounts of morality and don't grant empathy such a central role.

A LESS CENTRAL ROLL

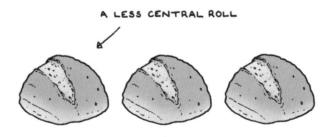

The position I'm offering you here is far from the most popular one—I just happen to think it's true.

I believe that empathy is the most likely candidate to be the kernel from which our kindness grows, because first, it's the explanation that provides the most accurate map for moral behavior; second, empathy explains kindness for kindness's sake; and third, it's the explanation that best matches the way kindness feels.

Take those accounts of morality under which we are kind because it's often rational for us to be so. If we interpret morality this way, our kindness must be born of whatever pushes us to behave rationally. However, what's rational for a person seems to depend on what that person desires. We can, I think, conceive of a person whose desires are such that for them it's perfectly rational to enact callous cruelty. Rationality doesn't tell us what to desire; it simply points to the most efficient means to achieve our preexisting ends.[2]

So, if rationality is the right explanation, we must either accept a strange, capricious account of morality under which the right thing to do for each person depends on what that person considers desirable, or we're left trying to explain how some pure form of rationality could motivate us all in the same direction, independent of what we each desire.[3]

In my view, many accounts of morality end up on the horns of an analogous dilemma: Either they don't match up with our understanding of what morality demands of us, or they have difficulty providing a satisfying account of our motivation to behave morally. It's easy to see, for example, that many of the rules and laws that people have relied on as moral systems are compatible with tremendous cruelty. So those who defend rule-based systems of morality must explain why their rules are the right ones, and how their rules are reliably and straightforwardly connected to people's motivation.

I don't deny we are sometimes kind because we're scared of breaking the rules, or because we're just in the habit of following them; or that we sometimes do the kind thing because we recognize that it's aligned with our interests, or because we want to be seen as doing the right thing. We can do what's right for all sorts of reasons that don't have much at all to do with kindness. But sometimes we are kind for kindness's sake; sometimes we are kind for no reason other than that it would feel wrong not to be, and surely this kind of kindness is the paradigmatic form.

KIND DUE TO
SELF-INTEREST
                          KIND OUT OF HABIT

   KIND OUT OF FEAR

(KIND BECAUSE IT FEELS RIGHT)

KIND IN CASE SOMEONE'S   KIND BY MISTAKE
WATCHING

                     KIND AS PART OF
   KIND DUE TO RULES   AN EXPERIMENT

PARADIGMATIC FORM OF KINDNESS

Some explanations of human kindness would require that we explain away kindness for kindness's sake. If the ultimate source of human kindness is that the rules instruct us to behave kindly, then our kindness would be conditional; we would be

kind only insofar as we recognized that kindness aligned with the rules of our society. That conditionality is incompatible with what we take kindness to be at its purest.

It feels wrong and strikes me as inaccurate to explain kindness in a way so disconnected from the way the pull of kindness feels. And it feels wrong to give a place in our account of morality to factors that we're loath to consider morally relevant, such as: Is anyone watching? Is this required by the rules? Is it rational to be kind in this case?

Explanations of our kindness that give a place to these types of contingencies cannot explain what we take kindness to be at its core; however, partaking in the pain and pleasure of others through our empathy can and does.

And that partaking in the pain and pleasure of others matches how it feels when you experience the pull to kindness. I can only speak for myself, but if I look inward while considering two courses of action, one kind and one cruel, and try to get a handle on what feeling is pushing me toward the former, I find that I'm sharing in the pain of those people my actions might affect; I'm empathizing. Ultimately, this is why I think empathy explains kindness and morality; the feeling that some course of action is wrong *just is* an empathy feeling.

WHAT MAKES YOU THINK THAT EMPATHY IS THE CORE OF MORALITY?

MORAL FEELINGS JUST ARE EMPATHY FEELINGS.

When I find myself deciding it would be wrong to pinch my neighbor's adorable puppies, however much I may want to, that decision—and my motivation to stick to it—is grounded in my empathizing with the sadness my neighbor would experience.

Similarly, when I try to convince my partner that it would be wrong for her to pinch our neighbor's adorable puppies—however much she may want to—I find, on introspection, that I am trying to appeal to that same empathetic feeling in her. I expect her to also empathize with our neighbor's imagined sorrow, and I'm asking her to act as that feeling pulls her to act. Morality has a distinctive feeling, and that feeling, as it happens, is empathy.

Only an empathetic account of morality captures the way we experience moral demands. You imagine some course of action, imagine how the people affected by that action might feel, experience some part of that feeling, and are then motivated (at least, to some extent) to act morally.

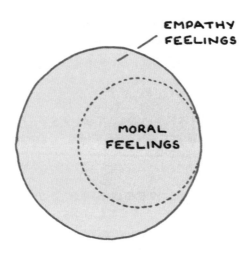

Empathy is the explanation of human kindness that best explains true kindness—kindness born from no ulterior motive—and it explains the way kindness feels. And, happily, it's an explanation that points the way to an expansion of our kindness.

You are kind thanks to empathy. You are not kinder only because your empathy is regularly limited. To make you kinder, we'll have to overcome those limits. We'll get to that, but first, in the next chapter, I'd like to explain how I know that you have empathy, and where it comes from.

3

Empathy evolved

The evolution of altruism

I know that you, the current reader of this book, have empathy, because every human does (barring, perhaps, individuals with psychopathy—although it's more likely they have reduced empathy than no empathy at all).

In fact, it's not just humans. We share this capacity with many of our closely related kin in the animal kingdom.

When a rat sees another rat stuck in a trap, she's willing to miss out on a chunk of chocolate to rescue her friend.[1] A dog can't hear another dog crying without wanting to offer some physical comfort.[2] And a rhesus monkey will forgo food and starve for several days if she must inflict an electric shock on another rhesus monkey to get at that food [3] (you might wonder about the empathetic capacity of whoever designed that last experiment).

I'M MAKING A CONSCIOUS
EFFORT TO TAKE UP
SPACE IN A SOCIETY
THAT PUNISHES
WOMEN FOR DOING SO.

We share empathy with many of our mammalian cousins and some birds because it's a product of evolution. Empathy is a near-universal feature of human nature because it evolved.[4]

Some of you, I'm sure, will have no problem accepting that. But some will point to the pithy slogans used to teach evolution by natural selection—phrases like "survival of the fittest" and "the selfish gene"—and will spot an apparent incompatibility between the evolutionary process and a pro-social motive like empathy. How, then, could a motive toward altruistic behavior evolve? Evolutionary biologists tend to rally around two answers to this question: kin selection and reciprocal altruism.

THIS PAIR OF JEANS
IS ONLY OUT FOR
ITSELF.

Kin selection is one of the theories proposed to explain how natural selection can favor those organisms that exhibit certain altruistic behaviors. It describes the possibility of selection for self-sacrifice when those behaviors are likely to be directed toward a close relative.

Our close relatives share many of our genes; therefore, in cases in which we can act to their advantage, even at great cost to ourselves, that behavior can evolve. A gene that predisposes you to act altruistically toward a biological sibling—a person with whom you share 50 percent of your genes—has a 50 percent chance of benefiting an identical gene carried by that sibling.[5]

HAMILTON'S RULE (NOT THAT HAMILTON)

ALTRUISM WILL BE FAVORED BY
NATURAL SELECTION WHEN

$$rB > c$$

(BASICALLY, NATURAL SELECTION
WOULD BE HAPPY FOR YOU TO
RISK YOUR LIFE TO SAVE TWO
BIOLOGICAL SIBLINGS, OR
EIGHT BIOLOGICAL COUSINS)

r = RELATEDNESS OF
THE ORGANISMS

B = BENEFIT TO THE
RECIPIENT

c = COST TO THE
ALTRUIST

Reciprocal altruism is another way to explain the evolution of apparently altruistic behaviors and motives. This theory provides a model for how and under what conditions behaviors can evolve that involve a sacrifice on the part of the actor to confer a greater benefit to someone else, where that benefit is likely to later be reciprocated.[6, 7]

During our evolutionary history, many situations must have arisen in which one or more organisms had a lot to gain if another would make some relatively minor sacrifice. Seemingly altruistic behaviors of this kind can be favored by natural selection if the actor will likely one day have that temporary sacrifice reciprocated (and can avoid being taken advantage of).

Here are two explanations of why—contrary to the popular right-wing imagining—natural selection needn't have produced animals with only an innate tendency toward selfishness (on top of which human civilization has painted a thin veneer of kindness[8]). In principle, evolution can produce altruistic behaviors and motives.

Evolution is a tinkerer

In the preceding section, I wanted to talk to readers who may have thought evolution and altruism are at odds, and who would therefore have immediately rejected the claim that empathy is an evolved feature of human nature. I hope the two theories briefly described go some way toward undermining that intuitive incompatibility.

But perhaps I've pushed some of you even further from accepting that empathy evolved. You may well have concluded that I've only shown that a mental algorithm ought to have

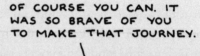

emerged to recognize kin and likely reciprocators, and to make humans dispense self-sacrificing behaviors only to the degree that would be evolutionarily advantageous.

You might think these mechanisms entail the evolution of humans who help out only close relatives and those they can guarantee will pay them back. And that doesn't match up with empathy as I've described it.

But this isn't exactly how evolution works.

It's important to recognize that understanding these two models, kin selection and reciprocal altruism, simply helps us to recognize the possibility that some altruistic behaviors evolved; it doesn't tell us exactly which traits, behaviors, emotions, and motives will have manifested that possibility.[9]

There are many ways to pet a cat, and there are many routes evolution might have taken to get us to be a bit altruistic. And in considering which behaviors might have evolved, in line with predictions from these theories, you've got to remember that evolution is a tinkerer, not a designer.

Evolution doesn't start with a blank blueprint each time it goes to work and try to design the required trait for some purpose from scratch, with a view to perfection. Evolution cobbles new features together from what it's created before, aiming not at perfection but at good enough—or rather, at better on average, in the long run, than the available alternatives.[10]

(Of course, evolution isn't conscious at all in the way this metaphor implies; it's an indifferent statistical process. However, where a metaphorical conscious creator is useful, the image of the tinkerer gets closer to the truth than that of the designer.)

While kin selection and reciprocal altruism theories point to the possibility of the evolution of limited forms of altruistic behavior, they don't tell us how the evolutionary tinkerer will have brought that altruistic behavior about, or how it will have thrown together those limits. What's more, the world in which evolution produced the traits we possess is very different from the world in which we currently exist. We were forged in an environment that existed tens of thousands of years ago; evolution has adapted us to a life unlike that which most of us now lead.

This can be seen clearly when it comes to our dietary preferences. In the environment to which we adapted, sugar was a rare and precious resource that evolution needed us to eagerly consume whenever we got the opportunity. There was little chance, during our hunter-gatherer existence, of too much sugar becoming a problem. However, in the modern world, that same taste for sugar can prove unhealthy for lots of us, because many of us now have access to as much sugar as we could ever want.

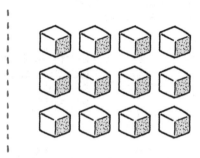

SUGAR AVAILABLE FOR
MILLIONS OF YEARS OF
EVOLUTIONARY HISTORY

SUGAR AVAILABLE TO
MANY OF US IN OUR
MODERN ENVIRONMENTS

Some of our evolved traits are adaptations to an environment that we no longer occupy.

The evolution of empathy's limits

Putting all this together, we can see that while it would have been ideal from an evolutionary perspective for humans to evolve a sort of internal computer program that accurately calculated exactly how much self-sacrifice it would be adaptive to dish out, this was unlikely to ever be an option available to evolution.

In the place of that ideal strategy, empathy—the capacity to share in and truly care about the feelings of others—was a good enough way to get us to be somewhat altruistic.

Of course, evolution also had to patch together some limits to our empathy. The theories of kin selection and reciprocal altruism don't point to the emergence of universal benevolence.

But what's crucial, going forward, is how exactly our empathy is limited. If evolution had managed to install that ideal program and it unfailingly shut down your empathy when it spotted someone who wasn't kin or a likely reciprocator, this book would have little chance of succeeding in its overarching aim of making you kinder.

Happily, that's not how our empathy is limited. Evolution found that it could rely on our ancestors' imperfect knowledge to provide the limits to our empathy (again, evolution didn't *find* anything because it isn't conscious, but you get me).

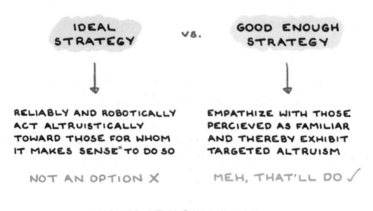

IDEAL STRATEGY vs. GOOD ENOUGH STRATEGY

RELIABLY AND ROBOTICALLY ACT ALTRUISTICALLY TOWARD THOSE FOR WHOM IT MAKES SENSE* TO DO SO

EMPATHIZE WITH THOSE PERCIEVED AS FAMILIAR AND THEREBY EXHIBIT TARGETED ALTRUISM

NOT AN OPTION ✗

MEH, THAT'LL DO ✓

*MAKES SENSE FROM THE METAPHORICAL PERSPECTIVE OF NATURAL SELECTION

In the environment in which empathy first evolved, the environment to which our empathy is adapted, we lived in small, stable groups composed largely of closely related family members. Evolution could count on our knowing very little about those who weren't members of that group.

So, evolution's strategy for limiting our empathy in accordance with the demands of kin selection and reciprocal altruism was to make sure our empathy failed when it came to those we knew little about. Evolution could depend on our ancestors knowing nothing about those who weren't members of their clan, and it used this as the workaround mechanism through which to direct their empathy. Empathizing only with those with whom they were familiar was probably an adequate mechanism for stopping our ancestors from empathizing with—and acting altruistically toward—those outside the group.

An empathy-limiting mechanism like this can be observed clearly in experiments on rats.[11] A white rat raised among only white rats will fail to empathize with a black rat; she will readily save another white rat from a trap but won't do the same for a black one. But a white rat raised only around black rats will fail to empathize with other white rats; she'll save black rats from the trap but won't do the same for white ones.

RAT COLOR	RAISED WITH	EMPATHIZES WITH

If you ran only the first experiment, it would appear as though rats empathize with those who look similar to them, but the truth is more of an evolutionary tinker than that. A rat's empathy is limited to those that look like the rats she grew up with. A white rat raised around black and white rats empathizes with, and acts to rescue, rats of both colors.

Evolution's aim may have been to limit rats' empathy to only those who belonged to their kin group, but its mechanism for achieving that was to engineer empathy to fail when faced with unfamiliar-looking rats.

Empathy evolved. And it evolved with limits. But thankfully, evolution fucked up (in a strictly metaphorical sense) when tinkering together those limits. It didn't restrict our empathy with hard, immovable walls; it relied on the soft limits of our knowledge to provide the limits to our empathy.

Our empathy fails when directed toward those we are unfamiliar with, those whose lives we know little about, and those we don't recognize as sharing in our emotional world. But when we learn about people, those empathy limits can crumble. We could, in principle, empathize far more widely than we currently do.

Empathy evolved the way it did because evolution could rely on human ignorance. But the ignorance that once reliably limited our ancestors' empathy isn't so easily maintained in the modern world.

4

Empathy has an off switch

Why aren't we kinder?

This book's supposed to make you kinder. Reintroducing you to your empathy, the source of that kindness, might have already had a bit of that titular effect.

Hopefully, you'll be taking empathy more seriously now, and listening for its call. Alongside that, you might be taking less seriously an alternative account of morality you accepted, which was justifying a limiting picture of your moral duties. And maybe, on its own, a belief in empathy as the kernel of kindness could help you make some marginal kindness gains.

But this book isn't about marginal kindness gains; it's about drastic ones. I'm thinking we've got room for a revolutionary expansion of kindness, and I'm hoping we can leap into it. So this book can't just get you to spend some time thinking about kindness and empathy; it has to argue you into greater kindness.

IF YOU MOVE TOO
FAST, YOU DON'T
NOTICE ALL THE
OPPORTUNITIES
THERE ARE TO
BE KIND.

I want this book to work even for the person who's currently thinking, "Yeah empathy forces me to be a bit kind. I'm glad it's limited; I wouldn't want to be any kinder."

We need a response for them too.

I don't want to just point at our kindness limits; I need to show that they're bad limits. I want to persuade you that action is required to challenge those limits, and that we'd be wrong—straightforwardly mistaken—to not do that work.

You are kind because of empathy. But why aren't you kinder? And why *should* you be kinder?

Empathy has an off switch, and that off switch is ignorance. Certain mistakes we have a tendency to make stop us from empathizing; making these mistakes can result in us seeing someone in pain and feeling no part of that pain. Ignorance is empathy's kryptonite; it leaves us insensitive to the suffering of those whose pain we would otherwise feel.

Mistakes limit empathy in three main ways:

1. They can leave us failing to recognize some individual (often by virtue of their group membership) as someone who feels in much the same way that we do.

2. They can give us an inaccurate picture of how people are feeling, or how they could feel in the future on the basis of actions we're considering.

3. They can hide the connection between our actions and the feelings of others.

Empathy's not unique in our emotional repertoire for having the potential to be influenced by our errors. Many of our feelings can be misdirected when our beliefs don't accurately reflect the world as it is. A false belief could, for example, misdirect your anger. Imagine one day noticing a new dent in your car. If you, like me, are carless, you will also have to imagine owning a car.

A GAY DUCK AND
A STRAIGHT DUCK
WALK INTO A BAR...
THEY HAVE A
GREAT TIME. DUCKS
NEVER DEVELOPED
HOMOPHOBIA.

Now imagine thinking your neighbor Kevin was responsible for the dent.

You'd be angry with Kevin, no doubt. Not only did he dent your car, he didn't have the courtesy to let you know and offer to pay to have the dent repaired. If you're British (as I am), you would, in this imagined scenario, keep your feelings to yourself and maintain a sort of festering resentment toward Kevin for the remainder of your relationship.

But then imagine that one day your other neighbor, Karen, confessed it was she who dented your car. Your anger toward Kevin in this situation was unfounded; it was misdirected. Your mistaken belief about the culprit in the denting left you with an anger toward Kevin you would otherwise not have felt.

This isn't an unusual phenomenon. We often find that the way we felt about something or toward someone was not the way we would have felt if we'd known more. And when we come to know more, our feelings tend to adjust. Our misdirected emotions can get back on track when we stop making the relevant mistake.

I hope it's uncontroversial to say you'd like to feel as you would if you weren't making any mistakes. You aim to feel, and thereby act, as the non-mistaken version of you would. And that is the crucial premise in my argument that you should be kinder: You don't want to feel a particular way because of a mistake.[1] If you grant me that, all that's left for me to do is convince you that there are currently some mistakes limiting your empathy.

Let's turn to empathy-limiting mistakes. What might they look like?

A straightforward example: You get on a bus and all the seats are taken, so you stand in the aisle. What you don't know is that you are standing on an elderly man's toe. He doesn't want to cause a scene or draw attention to himself on the bus, so he sits there in pained, stoic silence (you can tell all my examples are from Britain).

In this example, you don't know the man is in pain, and you don't know there is a connection between his pain and your actions. This is an empathy-limiting mistake; ignorance is switching your empathy off. If you were to learn that you were standing on his foot—perhaps another passenger notices and points it out—you'd empathize with his pain and recognize how easily you could end it.

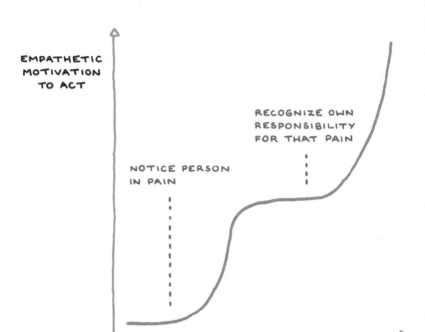

EMPATHETIC
MOTIVATION
TO ACT

RECOGNIZE OWN
RESPONSIBILITY
FOR THAT PAIN

NOTICE PERSON
IN PAIN

TIME

But this case is easy; the other passenger would have no trouble pointing out your error, and there would be no sacrifice on your part in simply moving your foot. Often it's harder to spot our own empathy-limiting mistakes, and more will be required from us when we do.

One of the most recognizable forms of an empathy-limiting mistake is our habit of hurting the people we love, because we don't realize we're doing so.

Let's say that when you were a teenager, your parent or primary caregiver took great pride in cooking a special, time-consuming meal every Sunday, and that working on this meal and sitting down together to eat it was one of the main ways they tried to express their love. Being a teenager, you might not

have recognized the work that went into that meal, or known what it was intended to express. Maybe, because of that lack of knowledge, you were regularly late to dinner, or distracted and distant when at the table.

In this imagined scenario (definitely not taken from my own life), you'd have caused pain in a way that you had no knowledge of. If you'd come to know a bit more, you would have felt differently; you'd have felt some empathetic motivation to take Sunday meals more seriously.

But in this example, spotting your mistake might not be as easy, and undoing the hurt caused will be trickier.

So, an empathy-limiting mistake is any mental state that would change in light of new, more accurate information, and would change in such a way that you would find yourself with a greater empathetic motivation to pursue a particular course of action. This kind of mistake is everywhere; it's the reason people so often fall short of the kindness we optimistically expect of them.

Some people no doubt (though they're unlikely to be among my readership) will want to respond that of course we turn off our empathy when it comes to strangers—of course we don't feel with those who are not our friends, family, or countrymen. Nothing can be more natural, they'll say, than the tendency for a primate to feel prosocial motivation when it comes to their "in-group" and to feel nothing of the sort when it comes to the "out-group."

The important thing to keep in mind is that in calling atten-

ARE YOU MOTIVATED TO
ACT A PARTICULAR WAY?

YES   NO

WOULD YOU BE   I'M SORRY, THAT'S
MOTIVATED TO ACT   SO DIFFICULT. I'VE
DIFFERENTLY IF YOU   BEEN THERE AND
KNEW MORE ABOUT   IT'S AN AWFUL
THE WORLD?   FEELING.

YES   NO

                         YOU'RE EITHER
                         OMNISCIENT OR
WOULD YOUR   ASLEEP.
NEWFOUND
MOTIVATION BE
EMPATHETIC IN
NATURE?

YES   NO

                         YOU ARE MAKING A
                         MISTAKE OF SOME
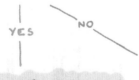   OTHER VARIETY.

YOU ARE MAKING AN
EMPATHY-LIMITING
MISTAKE.

tion to the naturalness of empathy, I am not claiming empathy is commendable because it is natural, and that therefore any natural limits on empathy must be celebrated for the same reason. (I talk about the evolution and innateness of empathy not to endorse it on that basis, but to explain why we can expect almost everyone to possess it, and why, therefore, no other explanation of human kindness is needed.)

It is a fallacy (known as the naturalistic fallacy) to claim that anything that can be shown to be natural is thereby shown to be morally good.

So, just because we may have a "natural" tendency toward more limited empathy when it comes to those we consider members of the out-group, we cannot jump directly to the conclusion that those limits are good or right. We must inquire (as we have) as to the mechanism through which those limits are implemented. Independent of their perceived naturalness, are they defensible limits?

100% NATURAL

100% PREDICATED
ON IGNORANCE

EMPATHY
OFF SWITCH

The question I would put to the proponent of maintaining empathetic walls around only those who are members of the right gang is this: Would you be able to limit your empathy so successfully if you knew as much about the out-group as you do about those you consider "in"? If you talked to those people outside what you take to be the boundaries of your moral duties (be that your family, community, or country), wouldn't you find it difficult to ignore their pain, as you think it right that you do? With every new humanizing nugget you learned about the out-group, wouldn't your empathy start overspilling its banks?[2]

Most people, were they honest with themselves, would recognize that their lack of empathy for outsiders (and their resultant belief that said lack of empathy is commendable) is dependent on their lack of knowledge about those outsiders. We do tend to empathize more readily with what we consider our in-group, but that's because we know more about them; the boundaries of that group rely on our ignorance of those left outside. Our empathy limits ought to be assessed on this basis, not on the question of their naturalness.

When we bar someone from the circle of our empathetic concern, we do so on the basis of ignorance, on the basis of mistakes, and for indefensible reasons. Our empathy limits— the empathetic distinction between in and out—are predicated on our getting something straightforwardly wrong.

Why *should* we be kinder? Because we don't like feeling or acting a specific way because of a mistake, and the only reason we aren't already kinder is that we're currently making some mistakes that have limited our empathy.

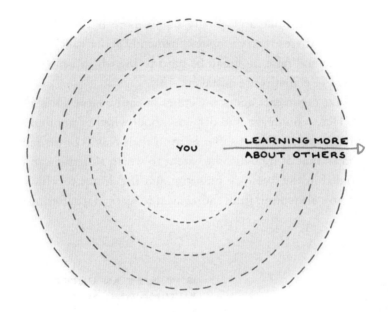

What is morality?

Many of the empathy-limiting mistakes that do the most harm are more difficult to recognize as mistakes than those in the examples I gave. No one's going to dispute that we shouldn't stand on an elderly man's toes, and that lots of us could afford to be kinder to our parents or primary caregivers. But more commonly, those areas of belief that might reduce or redirect one's empathy are highly contested.

We're often in disagreement when it comes to those beliefs about how our actions stand in relation to the experiences of others, how the world is currently experienced by members of certain groups, and how the world could be changed to reduce suffering (without accidentally doing more harm). When it comes to these areas, we argue vehemently about which beliefs are true and false, so it can be hard to say which beliefs that affect our empathy are mistaken.

Take arguments about the ethics of eating meat, for example. Here, you might find disputes about whether nonhuman animals are capable of suffering, or if their pain is of the same kind as that of humans; the extent to which suffering can be avoided in the livestock industry; and the degree to which a person's abstention from eating meat reduces that suffering.

IS IT JUST AN UNFEELING AUTOMATON, AS DESCARTES BELIEVED, AND THEREFORE INCAPABLE OF SUFFERING?

OR

IS IT LIKELY TO FEEL PAIN IN MUCH THE SAME WAY WE DO BECAUSE IT SHARES THOSE FEATURES OF OUR ANATOMY THOUGHT TO INSTANTIATE PAIN?

The beliefs formed in response to these disputes have a large impact on the way your empathy directs you to act, so it's worth taking care when forming beliefs in domains like this.

At their best, this is the role of moral and political arguments. In these arguments, we marshal facts and try to direct one another's attention to certain details in an effort to correct each other's empathy-limiting mistakes.

Under the view I'm presenting in this book (which, again, isn't one that many philosophers would back), when you argue about moral right and moral wrong with someone, you're trying to get them to recognize a mistake they've been making; you hope that if they spot that mistake and correct it, they will feel empathetically as you do, and act differently.

At the start of the book I said that along with making you kinder, I'd be trying to explain what morality even is. I suggested that morality is the domain of thought in which we explore which kindnesses and abstentions from cruelty we ought to be able to expect from one another. We can now narrow that down further.

I believe moral facts are facts about what your empathy would motivate you to do if you were making no mistakes that affected it.

So I'm proposing that saying some action is morally right is equivalent to saying, "If you were making no mistakes, you would be motivated by empathy to act in that way."

We'll sometimes disagree on which empathy-affecting beliefs are true and which are false, which means we'll sometimes disagree on how our empathy would look if we were the wholly non-mistaken versions of ourselves. In my view, that's what's at stake in arguments about morality.

Culpable ignorance and comfortable beliefs

Under the account given here of what limits kindness, mistaken beliefs should explain a large part of our cruelty. I've claimed that our unkindness is usually the result of mistakes we make about purely factual matters. But what I really don't want to imply is that we are always blameless when we make an empathy-limiting mistake, that no one could ever be at fault for acting cruelly because they only do so out of ignorance. I am decidedly not saying and do not believe that the ignorance that precipitates our unkindness is something for which we have no responsibility.

It's important in talking about these empathy-limiting mistakes that we keep in mind a distinction between culpable and inculpable forms of ignorance.

IGNORE ANTS

Sometimes, you make a mistake and you genuinely couldn't have known better. You didn't know you were the cause of some harm, and when you learned that you were, you quickly

changed how you acted. This is what we'd call inculpable ignorance, and standing on someone's toe on a crowded bus and genuinely not noticing would be a good example of it.

But sometimes, we're ignorant in empathy-limiting ways and we could—and should—have known better. This is what we'd call culpable ignorance.

Say in the case of the lovingly cooked Sunday dinner, you wanted to skip it because you'd been invited to a party. Let's imagine you'd managed to convince yourself, through self-deceit, that no one would feel very strongly about you missing the dinner because believing this made it easier for you to sneak off. That would be culpable ignorance on your part. You worked at not imagining the consequences of your actions, not coming to the straightforward conclusion that all the preparatory work likely meant that the dinner meant something; and you did so precisely because you didn't want to spend the party picturing your parent or primary caregiver's sorrow.

We're often culpable for forming those beliefs that turn our empathy off. We're culpable when we could have known better, and particularly when we formed those beliefs precisely because they turned our empathy off. Our beliefs have an impact on the empathy we experience, but those beliefs are by no means formed in a vacuum, entirely prior to the act of empathizing. We don't believe first and feel second; our beliefs and our feelings are formed in a sort of ongoing loop.

There's always a temptation to believe what it's comfortable to believe. And when it comes to those beliefs connected to empathy, it will often be most comfortable to believe that which switches empathy off. It can be comfortable to believe there aren't many people suffering, or that our actions have no impact on the suffering of others. But where those beliefs are false, and we could have known they were false, we are responsible for getting it wrong. The more dire the consequences of our mistakes, the greater our duty to avoid those mistakes.

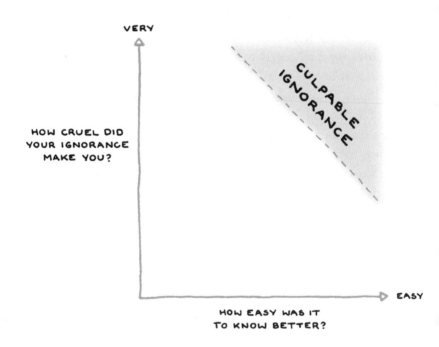

Going forward, I'm going to talk about some widespread examples of empathy-limiting mistakes, and it's important to me that as I explain people's unkindness, you don't interpret me as trying to explain it away. I believe that we are able to act cruelly only when we make certain types of errors, but in explaining cruelty in this way I'm not aiming to let anyone off the hook.

People make these mistakes in part because they want to act in the way that the mistake allows them to.

We've arrived at an account of why we are kind and why we aren't kinder. We are kind thanks to empathy, and our kindness is limited to the extent it is because we make certain mistakes that switch empathy off. But this book will make you drastically kinder only if it helps you to spot and correct a lot of your own empathy-limiting mistakes.

In chapter 6, we'll explore some examples of empathy-limiting mistakes, but in the next chapter I'd like to talk about why those mistakes are distributed as they are, so we know where to start looking for them.

WHY DO SOME HUMANS
PREFER THE COMPANY
OF DOGS TO THAT
OF OTHER HUMANS?

A DOG HAS NEVER
SHAMED A HUMAN
FOR BEING THEIR
AUTHENTIC SELF.

5

The unequal distribution of empathy-limiting mistakes

It turns out empathy-limiting mistakes don't fall evenly. It's not the case that everyone is as likely as everyone else to be the subject of botched empathy. And it's important that as we start trying to spot our own unkindness, we think about why that is.

This book isn't saying that we have all been failing at empathy to the same extent, and that we all suffer to the same degree because of those failings. We have not and we do not.

I fear that a wealthy, thin, nondisabled, cis, straight, white man could give this book a brief skim and think, "Yeah, this chap is so right—everyone should know more about my experiences, and empathize with my feelings a bit more."

That is not at all my point.

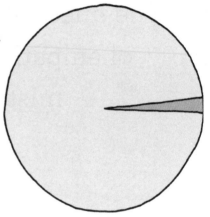

THE MESSAGE I WANT YOU TO TAKE FROM THIS BOOK

(PARTICULARLY IF YOU'RE HIGHLY PRIVILEGED)

☐ I SHOULD EMPATHIZE MORE WITH EVERYONE ELSE

☑ EVERYONE SHOULD EMPATHIZE MORE WITH ME

Sure, everyone probably has a bit of room to expand their empathy, but the empathy deficit in our society is distributed just as unevenly as everything else. The problem is not that oppressed people don't empathize enough with their oppressors; the problem is that privileged folk don't empathize enough with the oppressed (and that those categories exist in the first place; their existence is both a product and a major source of empathy-limiting mistakes).

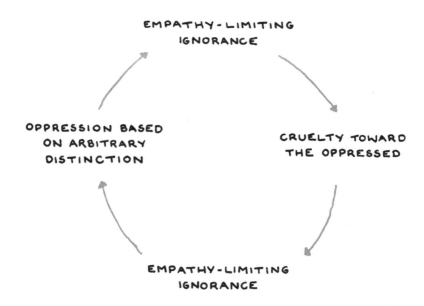

EMPATHY-LIMITING
IGNORANCE

OPPRESSION BASED
ON ARBITRARY
DISTINCTION

CRUELTY TOWARD
THE OPPRESSED

EMPATHY-LIMITING
IGNORANCE

The demand for greater empathy must be directed primarily toward those born to privilege. The reason for this is that privilege and oppression play a crucial role in the dissemination of knowledge; those with privilege are predisposed to certain types of empathy-limiting ignorance.[1]

Privilege filters the experiences of those who benefit from it. It hides from their immediate view the many social cruelties from which it shields them.[2] Those on the violent end of an axis of oppression are made to develop a comprehensive expertise on that oppression and the many ways in which it manifests. But those at the privileged end of that axis are afforded the luxury of ignorance. They don't have to learn about other people's oppression; the world doesn't force them to.

In fact, in many ways, other people's oppression is actively hidden. Part of the privilege of being cis, for example, is that because cis people are not the targets of transphobia, they don't have the same need to learn of its prevalence.

Privilege shapes the way we perceive the world. A disabled person and a nondisabled person can enter the same room and see two entirely different spaces.[3] If the disabled person is a wheelchair user, they'll instantly spot narrow gaps and short flights of stairs that may be invisible to their privileged counterparts.

The wheelchair user has a deep, lived knowledge of the way a wheelchair interacts with the room that the nondisabled person may not. But it is only with that knowledge that one's empathy can be switched fully on.

Knowledge of this kind is available to those of us with privilege—the privilege of not having to learn doesn't mean we can't learn. But we don't learn by default, through painful experiences, the same way oppressed people are made to[4] (this socially enabled ignorance creates a duty for privileged folk to listen; we'll return to that later).

And it's not just that privilege filters experiences on an individual level; it also encourages ignorance at a structural one. To see why, we need to talk about power, that attribute of individuals, groups, and their relationships that gives some people a greater ability to access and control resources as well as the lives of others.

Power is often broken down conceptually into "power to" and "power over."[5] Power to might be exemplified by the power white people have to walk down the street holding a water pistol without risking police violence, while power over can be illustrated by the power colonizers exert over colonized people by deeming certain practices barbaric, to socially and legally suppress those practices (before later appropriating them for their own entertainment).

Power is distributed unevenly in our society.

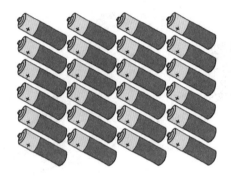

At the individual and structural levels, some groups have more power than others, as shown by their overrepresentation in well-paid, high-status jobs and institutions of state power; their ability to carry out the normal functions of daily life without the risk of violence; the ways in which bodies like theirs are presented as the norm and catered to by public spaces; and the relative impunity with which they can commit infractions that are severely punished when committed by members of other groups.

Power is relevant for our purposes because it determines which stories get told. It is those with power—those who own the newspapers, publishing houses, and production companies, those who write the history books and work as professors and researchers— who decide who gets to tell their own story, on their own terms, and which stories will be believed and amplified.

THE NEWS — THINGS AREN'T AS BAD FOR WOMEN AS THEY CLAIM SAYS ONE MAN

By default, in this society, we hear only certain types of stories. Only particular groups of people have the power to communicate their lived experience. And those same people hold storytelling power over others: They hold the power to tell stories that are not their own, and the power to frame other people as deceptive when they try to reclaim their own narrative.

Put simply, we are far more likely to hear the first-person life story of a straight white man than of a Black lesbian;[6] we are more likely to hear an account of sex work from someone who hasn't worked in that industry than from someone who has;[7] and those who falsely believe that trans women are a threat to cis women are more able to share their belief than those who recognize its falsehood.[8]

You don't need to believe in some well-planned conspiracy to recognize that the first line of defense for the current power structure is this power over stories. The dominant group tends to defend and justify that unjustifiable dominance, and they do so by controlling knowledge—by engineering useful,

GIVE A MAN A FISH AND
HE WILL DEVELOP A TASTE
FOR THAT FISH SO
VORACIOUS THAT HE WILL
DESECRATE ENTIRE
ECOSYSTEMS IN PURSUIT
OF MORE OF THAT FISH.

comforting, false beliefs; by promoting ignorance of suffering and inequality of power; by limiting people's imagination; and by providing moral rationalization for their cruelty. And everyone who has a stake in power—everyone who is a member of the dominant group—is incentivized to maintain this justificatory obliviousness.[9]

STORYTELLING
POWER

=

POWER TO CONVEY   +   POWER OVER THE
OWN NARRATIVE   NARRATIVES OF
                                    OTHERS

The vast majority of the mistakes and the cruelty that can be said to be socially conditioned are the product of privilege.

What's more, powerful people's failures to empathize have more dire consequences than similar failures of oppressed people ever could. This is another reason inequalities of power are so fundamental in bringing about large-scale cruelty: If it weren't for some groups having power over the lives of others, failures to empathize wouldn't cause nearly as much harm. Failing to recognize and partake in someone else's pain becomes a far more serious problem when you have power over that person's life.[10]

This point about exactly who needs to step up their empathy game is made all the more vital because demands for greater empathy have, in fact, frequently been weaponized against the oppressed, as a form of spiritual bypassing.

Spiritual bypassing is a derailing method often used by white people when Black people hold them accountable for racism or even simply point out its existence. Public academic, writer, and anti-racist educator Rachel Elizabeth Cargle describes the way many white people, when confronted with the harm they have done, evade the conversation by appealing to a need for "unity, love, and peace."[11]

This technique for derailing a conversation about accountability works by framing the person who is justifiably angry about racism as equally culpable for the tarnished unity as the person who has been racist. The anger about the initial racism is now the problem to be solved, not the racism itself.

The word *empathy* has also been (mis)used as a form of spiritual bypassing. Those with power are all too ready, when held to account, to appeal to a need for greater "empathy" among all people. This appeal for empathy is an instance of spiritual bypassing: Rather than the privileged party attempting to spot the limitations on their own empathy, they attempt to frame all parties as equally culpable for a widespread lack thereof.

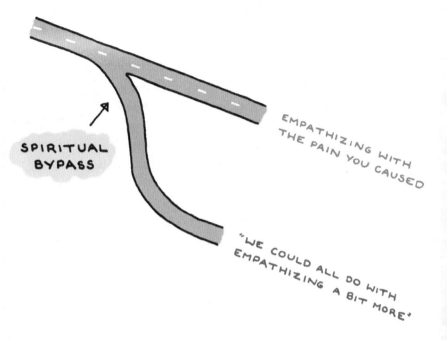

SPIRITUAL BYPASS

EMPATHIZING WITH THE PAIN YOU CAUSED

"WE COULD ALL DO WITH EMPATHIZING A BIT MORE"

This use of the word *empathy* serves as a cover for all manner of sins.[12] It's a cop-out and a distraction. To weaponize the concept of empathy in this way represents a failure to truly engage with its meaning and the usual reasons for its absence.

I'm not saying that oppressed folk are immune to empathy-limiting mistakes. But I am saying that power is a petri dish for these mistakes, and it makes their consequences far worse, so that's where the work must always start.

In the next chapter, I plan to introduce some examples of the different types of empathy-limiting mistakes we tend to make. I put the privilege chat we've just had here in hopes that those of us who hold particular forms of privilege will have an eye to where our own mistakes are more likely to crop up.

POWER

SIDE EFFECTS INCLUDE: EMPATHY-LIMITING IGNORANCE, ENTITLEMENT TO SPACE, VIOLENCE, CORRUPTION, RESPONSIBILITY

6

Mistakes that
can turn empathy off

Have you ever ordered in a restaurant and only then noticed the specials board?

Recently, I was sitting there pretty satisfied with my choice of pizza, when I noticed a chalkboard out of the corner of my eye, and there in faded chalky writing (among some unappealing experiments with the calzone form) was the option of a special pizza topped with garlicky roasted potatoes.

Of course, had I known that there was a carb-on-carb option available, that's what I would've ordered. If I'd had more knowledge of that pizza restaurant, I would have felt differently; I would have felt an overwhelming desire for potatoes on my pizza.

This disastrous pizza trip reminds me of my early experiences with feminism. Just like my ignorance of the pizzas available, my ignorance of the experiences of women and folk of other marginalized genders resulted in me feeling differently than I would have felt had I known more. While in the former case, my ignorance thwarted a desire I would've had for a different pizza, in the latter, my mistakes stopped me from empathizing as I now do (I don't want to sound complacent; I still have a lot to learn, and I'm certain that I will come to recognize further gaps in my knowledge).

My mistakes regarding feminism are mistakes for which I'm culpable. It wasn't my fault that I didn't notice the specials board in a dimly lit corner of that restaurant, and it only harmed me. However, it was my fault that I listened to the cis, straight, white, male comedians loudly shouting, "What more do these women want?" rather than the feminist campaigners highlighting an epidemic of sexual violence perpetrated overwhelmingly by cis men, and pointing out all the work left to do.[1]

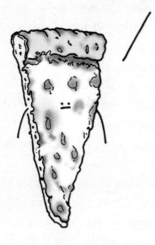

Because I made those mistakes, because I wasn't aware (because I chose not to listen) of what it's like to be a person oppressed on the basis of gender in the society in which I live, I didn't empathize with the suffering caused by our sexist culture, to which I was contributing.

I wasn't motivated to get involved in that movement—feminism—that seeks to bring an end to that suffering, but I would have been if I'd known more. My empathy was limited by a mistake, and it's a mistake I'm responsible for having made.

But this book isn't just about me; it's about us all, and the many forms of cruelty we perpetrate.

You are currently making some empathy-limiting mistakes. Again, this isn't a dig at you; I doubt there's anyone who isn't. We've never met (or maybe we have—"Hi, Mum!"), so I don't know exactly which mistakes you're making. But our ignorance tends to follow certain patterns. Many of us limit empathy in the exact same ways.

So, while I can't tell from where I'm typing precisely what's turning your empathy off, I can give you a sort of taxonomy of some common forms of ignorance. My hope is that this list will help you spot and undo some of your own empathy-limiting mistakes; maybe you've been making some of those listed, or perhaps the list and its structure will help you to notice your own related errors.

YOU - IGNORANCE

=

YOU, BUT KINDER

I'm hoping it will function a bit like a Pokédex of our insensitivities.

False beliefs can switch our empathy off

Our first group of empathy-limiting mistakes is false beliefs. Believing something that isn't true can turn your empathy off toward a group or an individual.

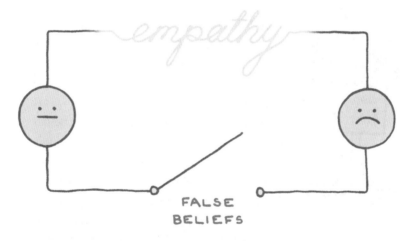

For example, if you believed that people wearing purple hats can't feel any pain, you might be tempted to place a purple hat on the head of someone whose toe you were accidentally standing on, rather than simply stepping off their toe.

Beliefs of this sort—beliefs that some subset of humans, usually picked out by their religious belief or membership in some racialized grouping, are insensible to suffering—have been instrumental in some of humanity's greatest atrocities.

Often, the relevant empathy-limiting belief isn't that some group doesn't feel anything at all, but that their feelings are so different from the in-group's as to make them alien and unrecognizable. In this context, dehumanization and "othering" play crucial roles.[2] If you believe that certain people don't experience feelings the same way you do, you can watch members of that group experience pain—and even cause them to experience pain—and feel nothing. The empathy you would have otherwise felt, and that would have compelled you to act differently, is thwarted.

And I know I'm going on about it, but that's because it's vital. Beliefs that particular people are devoid of feelings don't just accidentally appear from nowhere, and we are far from guiltless when we hold them. Beliefs like this gain traction or are deliberately engineered precisely because they are so comfortable to believe when one group is practicing large-scale cruelty against another. We are particularly culpable for our mistaken beliefs when they have devastating consequences.

Another group of beliefs that can have you witnessing pain and failing to empathize properly are beliefs that the pain is unavoidable.

If you believe, say, that poverty—and the suffering it causes—is a sad but inescapable side effect of the only tenable economic system, you might switch off your empathy for the

YOU'RE DIFFERENT FROM
OUR SHEEP PEERS AND YOUR
CLOTHING MARKS YOU OUT
EVEN FURTHER. IT WILL BE
EASY TO HOLD YOU RESPON-
SIBLE FOR EVERYTHING THAT
GOES WRONG, CAPE-GOAT.

pain of a child's empty belly or the fear of a parent who hears the bailiffs at the door.[3]

Our beliefs about the inevitability of certain forms of suffering are intimately connected with our beliefs about what type of world is possible. It's comfortable for those of us born into privileged positions in society to believe that utopian visions for how the world could be changed for the better are impossible to bring about in reality. Believing that our society could be altered to drastically reduce suffering would require empathy with pain that's been sidelined as unavoidable. It's much more comfortable to believe that nothing can be done, that only worlds that look fairly similar to the current one are possible.

WELL SURE, IT'D BE GREAT IF EVERYONE COULD HAVE A HOME, HEALTH CARE, AND ENOUGH TO EAT, BUT IT'S NOT REALISTIC!

WE WON'T KNOW UNTIL WE TRY.

So, false beliefs can help you to deny, reframe, and justify suffering of which you're aware. But they can also help hide suffering from your view, and disguise the connection between your actions and the suffering of others.

Rape myths are a group of widely held demonstrably false beliefs that contradict, minimize, or obscure the realities of rape and sexual violence. Rape myths take many forms and always have empathy-limiting consequences. One group of rape myths that curtail empathy by helping to hide certain people's suffering from view are those that concern how a survivor reacts to sexual violence.[4]

Many believe that a person who has been raped will have fought back, said no at least once, and shouted and screamed if there were people likely to hear; they also believe that after experiencing rape a person will immediately go to the police, would never appear friendly to the perpetrator again, and would be unlikely to be very sexually active in the future. These are all rape myths—false beliefs about how a survivor is likely to act.

For instance, the belief that someone who was "really" being raped would certainly fight back is based on people's (usually men's) uninformed assumptions about what they would do in those circumstances. Only learning about trauma responses—that it's very common to freeze up when experiencing trauma (an automatic, physiological response)—could disabuse a person of that belief.[5, 6]

As a matter of empirical fact, these beliefs about what a survivor of rape will do are false. Survivors respond in varied ways, many of which seem counterintuitive. But few people understand the effects of trauma, or the choices people make after

IT'S NOT ABOUT WANTING
TO HURT OUTSIDERS. I'M
JUST PROTECTIVE OF
THIS SPECIFIC PART OF
THE OCEAN.

I CAN SEE RIGHT
THROUGH YOU!

sexual violence to keep themselves safe and as mentally stable as possible.

Many survivors don't behave as someone who has experienced rape is expected to.[7] Thanks to these rape myths—these socially engineered false beliefs—their behavior is seen as evidence that they were not raped.[8] The majority of sexual violence is hidden from most people's view either by these beliefs or by the fact that due to these beliefs, many survivors never feel safe enough to publicly disclose their experience. Through this obfuscation, rape myths switch people's empathy off toward the majority of those who have experienced sexual violence.

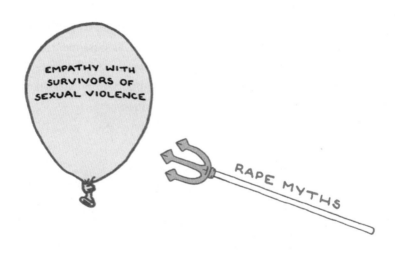

Beliefs like this—beliefs that serve to discredit the testimony of the disempowered, or that frame particular groups as more likely to be deceptive—are often weaponized to prevent those who are suffering from communicating their experiences.

These beliefs further enable the privileged in maintaining our ignorance.

Even an awareness of how everyone currently feels isn't guard enough against empathy-limiting mistakes; we can also hold mistaken beliefs about the connection between how we act and how others feel. If you can think of a time you've believed you were doing something completely harmless and only later learned of the pain it caused, you have in mind an example of just this.

To do the right thing, we're sort of required to predict the future. We have to imagine, as accurately as possible, the impact of the choices available to us. But we can get these predictions wrong—we can hold false beliefs about our impact on the world—and we can be culpable for doing so.

PREDICTED HARM
OF MY ACTION

MISSING EMPATHY

ACTUAL HARM
OF MY ACTION

If we're under the impression that someone's hurt is unrelated to our actions—that we're in no way complicit in that hurt and there's nothing we're failing to do that could end it—and it turns out that's not the case, we've made a mistake that's

JIMMY GOT CAUGHT IN A
SPIDERWEB, BUT I'D
SWEAR THERE WASN'T
ONE THERE.

SADLY PETE, SPIDERWEBS
ARE LIKE RACISM. THEY
DON'T DISAPPEAR JUST
BECAUSE YOU DENY
THEIR EXISTENCE.

torpedoed our empathy. The same is true whenever we go about trying to avert suffering in a way that backfires and causes even more; the failure to properly predict the consequences of our actions misdirects our empathy. This often occurs when a privileged group's beliefs about the best way to help have been shaped by their privilege-induced ignorance (I'm thinking particularly here of the white savior phenomenon[9]).

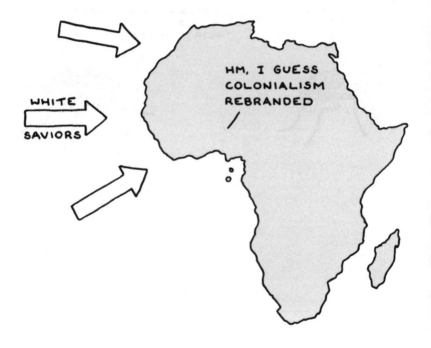

Maybe you're starting to think about all the empathy-limiting false beliefs you can spot in the world around you. Some that spring to my mind include the beliefs that homeless people are homeless because they choose to be; that people migrate across your nation's border to access the welfare state, not to flee danger; that older people can't hold politically progressive views; and that we live in a post-racial, color-blind society (so anyone who says otherwise must be lying or making trouble).[10]

(None of these false beliefs would actually justify cruelty toward the relevant group, even if they were true—that's definitely not what I'm claiming. My claim is only that beliefs of this kind are instrumental in enabling people to behave cruelly.)

On a more personal level, you could falsely believe that one of your friends is so mentally resilient that he couldn't possibly be quietly suffering from depression; that your sister was telling the truth when she told you she didn't need a birthday present this year; or that not halting your phone call when you reach the front of the checkout line has no effect on the day of the person serving you.

Perhaps you believe none of the above, but some other related falsehood, more difficult to spot and all the more intractable for it. But don't doubt for a moment that we all hold some mistaken beliefs that limit our empathy. We would be kinder than we are if these beliefs were corrected.

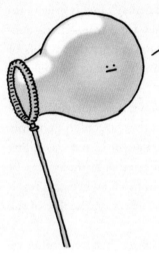

Not knowing enough
can switch our empathy off

Your empathy can be limited when you believe things that aren't true, but also when you don't know things that are. Not knowing enough about the experiences of someone or some group, or about how your actions impact their experiences, can switch your empathy off.

Perhaps it can't hurt you, but what you don't know is often what causes you to hurt others.

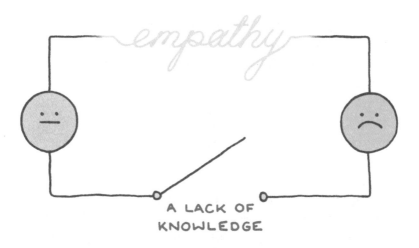

A LACK OF
KNOWLEDGE

Let's imagine you're part of a close friendship group, and one day, as part of some cute inside joke, you and some of your friends assign each member of that gang an animal-themed nickname; you take to calling one of your friends Rabbit and another Lion. But now imagine that one of your friends, who wasn't there that day but is now commonly referred to as Dog, was the victim of a traumatic incident in their childhood in which several dogs attacked them.

You and your friends don't know about the attack, but each time someone calls to them, "Hey, Dog!" they experience a moment of panic and return to the horror of that moment.

In this example, you act as you do only because of your ignorance of your friend's experience. If you'd known just a little bit more, you wouldn't have done so, because you would have been able to imagine and empathize with the suffering caused by that nickname.

It would have been difficult in this case for you to know any better. We wouldn't want to describe your motives as cruel; your ignorance was so unavoidable that no one is really culpable for your friend's suffering.

But this does point us to another group of empathy-limiting mistakes that we often are culpable for making. One way in which a lack of knowledge frequently limits your empathy is when you are ignorant of the context in which you are acting. Context matters. And it's often privilege that makes people blissfully unaware of the morally relevant context of their actions.

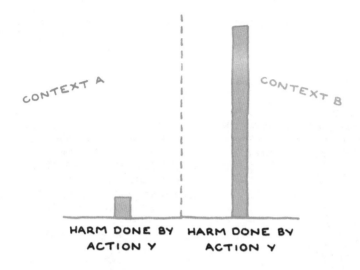

CONTEXT A   CONTEXT B

HARM DONE BY   **HARM DONE BY**
ACTION Y   **ACTION Y**

White people, for example, tend to be ignorant of the racial context in which our actions take place. One illustrative microcosm of this lack of knowledge I've learned about recently is the frequent request white people make to touch Black women's hair.[11, 12] The average white person knows very little about the context in which this dynamic plays out (and we're culpable for that ignorance). White people are far less likely to know the history of Black women's relationship with their hair: how its texture serves as a racial marker comparable in salience to skin color; the cultural meaning of the time and energy that can go into its maintenance; how shaving it was a common form of violence during slavery; and the role hair has played in the broader policing, objectification, and control of Black women's bodies—through discriminatory workplace and school dress

IT'S GOOD THAT YOUR HUMAN HAD A DOCTOR FRIEND TO TALK TO ABOUT YOUR PAIN.

I DID THINK IT WAS STRANGE THAT HE ASKED FOR MY GENDER, AND FUR COLOR, BEFORE HE DECIDED HOW SERIOUSLY TO TAKE IT.

codes that prohibit distinctly Black styles, and through dominant white standards of beauty against which Black women are judged.[13, 14]

The broader, hidden context here is a racist, sexist society that stereotypes Black and white femininity in diametrically opposed ways, and within that, media that simultaneously render Black women invisible and exotic.

In any context, asking to touch someone's hair would be a bit odd, but only knowledge of this specific context—in which Black women receive this same request over and over, making them feel hyper visible, serving to other them, and making it clear that it's part of a pattern of entitlement to their bodies—allows one to recognize the true harm of that request when directed at a Black woman.

Often privileged folk can't see the cumulative harm done by microaggressions like this. They get to be aware only of their own actions, and not those of the many other people like them who have needled the same person in the same way over a lifetime. A white person can easily (but culpably) believe that their "one-off" hair touching must be harmless, but it's through accumulation, and connection with many other experiences of racism, that these aggressions do their damage.

As a rule, when we benefit from a particular form of privilege, we're less likely to recognize the context in which we're acting. Just as white people tend to be ignorant of the context in which Black people exist, straight folk are ignorant of the queerphobic context in which their actions and words land. Privilege makes it more likely that we will fail to know in all kinds of empathy-limiting ways (for reasons briefly discussed in chapter 5).

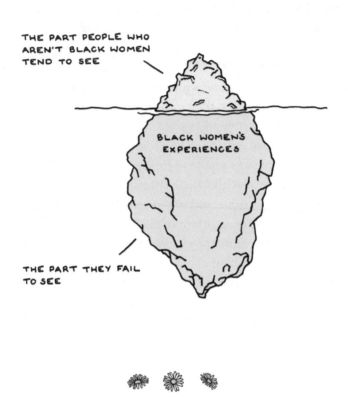

THE PART PEOPLE WHO AREN'T BLACK WOMEN TEND TO SEE

BLACK WOMEN'S EXPERIENCES

THE PART THEY FAIL TO SEE

This form of empathy-limiting mistake, the tendency for our empathy to be sabotaged by our lack of knowledge about other people's lives and our impact on them, accounts for the larger part of human cruelty. You can see this most clearly if you think about the opposite: those times when your empathy has been expanded by simply learning more about someone else. How often have you come to behave differently because you've talked to someone and realized that your actions were hurting them?

A simple example: Last summer, my dad asked me to remove the weeds from his overgrown garden. I know less than nothing about horticulture, but I enjoyed stomping round the flower beds pulling up those plants that, to my eye, looked out of place. So I was alarmed when dad came outside with his coffee, proudly chatting to my brother about the patch of chives he'd successfully cultivated.

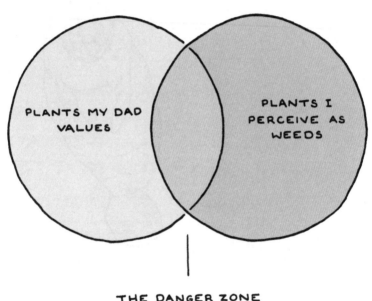

PLANTS MY DAD VALUES

PLANTS I PERCEIVE AS WEEDS

THE DANGER ZONE

That day I didn't have enough knowledge of which plants my dad values—for my future reference, chives are among them. As it turns out, one man's weeds are another man's cherished crops. When I learned more, I empathized more accurately with the feelings that my reckless style of gardening caused; I take more care now (but I'm rarely asked to garden anymore).

As painfully, face-blushingly guilty as dwelling on that moment has me feeling, the consequences of analogous forms of obliviousness are usually far more dire. We cannot empathize with suffering of which we are unaware, whether it's currently occurring or a future result of choices we make.

It's not only our lack of knowledge about suffering we cause directly that limits our empathy—often we fail to empathize with the consequences of cruelty perpetrated in our name. When you don't act to undo social injustices from which you benefit, you are just as responsible as if you had wrought that cruelty yourself. But suffering we cause in this less direct way is suffering we're even more likely to be ignorant of.

For my part, I've recognized in the past few years countless socially encouraged gaps in my knowledge of others (and I know that I'll come to see many more). My mind is like an atlas of the social world that has been scribbled on by a petulant youngster, obscuring every page that discusses lives unlike my own.

I'm only now learning, for example, of the role fatphobia plays in the lives of fat people, the failure of public spaces to accommodate nonnormative bodies, the violence and harassment they face, and the way in which these are reinforced by the disingenuous health concerns many of us convey.[15] It's only

YOU RESCUE DOGS ARE
ALL TOO SENSITIVE.
IT CAN'T BE THAT BAD.

WITHOUT EXPERIENCING
WHAT I HAVE, YOU'RE
ILL-PLACED TO JUDGE
WHETHER OR NOT I'M
BEING TOO SENSITIVE.

in my adult life that I've even learned that trans folk truly exist, and I'm only beginning to understand the consequences of existing at the intersection of trans, Black, and women's oppression,[16] and the ways in which those of us who are socially privileged benefit from the oppression of others.[17]

I can see so many ways in which my lack of knowledge has limited my empathy.

Without knowledge of other people's feelings and the causal connections between our actions and those feelings (particularly as those actions are mediated through the context of our wider society and people's past experiences), we cannot empathize as we would if we knew a little more.

There will always be gaps in our knowledge, but where those gaps hide people's pain from us, or hide our complicity in causing that pain, we have a duty to avoid blissful ignorance. If we hold tight to that ignorance, we're insisting on flailing dangerously in the moral dark.

Failures of imagination can switch our empathy off

But look, even in the absence of false beliefs, and with good knowledge of all the relevant lived experiences, our empathy can be limited when our imagination fails. To empathize in a fully non-mistaken way, we've not only got to know all the relevant facts of the matter, we've also got to vividly imagine the causal series of events that can be brought about through our actions.

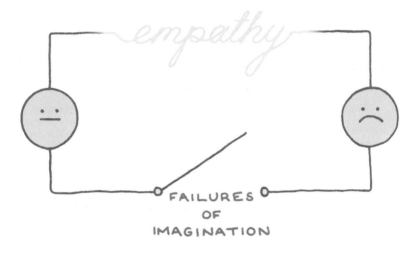

Let's say you desperately want a cookie, and someone has placed a plate of cookies on a table in your workplace—let's say they're really savory, slightly salty chocolate chip cookies with a hint of vanilla, because those are my favorites and I'm inventing the scenario. But you can see that whichever dastardly scientist put the cookies there, along with a little sign reading, "Please take one," has attached each of them by a strand of fishing line to a huge Rube Goldberg machine.

If you took a cookie, it would set off a contrived domino effect constructed from office paraphernalia. Imagine you can see the whole machine and can work out what each part of it is likely to do. You can see that the bulldog clips will fall on the photocopier button, and the photocopied sheets of paper will push over the precariously balanced folding chair, which will redirect the fan, and so on, and so on.

But the contraption is so big and so comically convoluted that you can't imagine what the
consequences of grabbing a
cookie will ultimately be. So
you take one. And it turns out
that the Rube Goldberg machine ends with a stack of
files falling on the handle of
a fire extinguisher, which
sprays foam all over your
long-suffering intern.

Had you imagined the whole series of cause and effect all
the way through, from your cookie grab to the spray of foam,
you would probably have left the cookies well alone. And while
I'm sure your life is largely free of cheeky scientists, I'm also
sure that those of us who interact with the global market economy spend our lives triggering gigantic Rube Goldberg networks in the form of global supply chains, the machinations of
which are nearly impossible to imagine.[18]

Often, when you buy things or refrain from doing so, the
causal routes between your actions and the consequences for
someone else are long, slow, and convoluted. To be motivated
by empathy to act a certain way, we've got to imagine how acting
that way will affect others, and imagine the experiences of those
affected. But when the action is buying something from a big
business, to picture the lived consequences of that choice you'd
have to be able to picture how that purchase will be converted
through an international web of economic signals into, perhaps,
a change in demand for the labor of someone who lives on the
other side of the world.

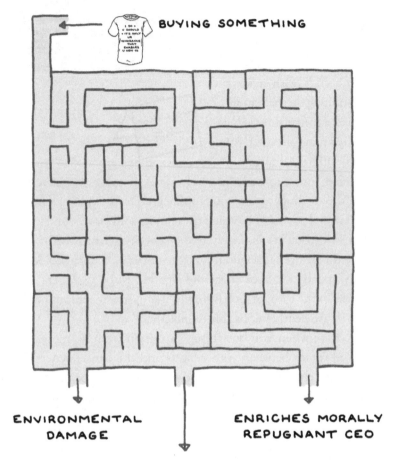

We're all aware, on some level, that how we spend money can cause or mitigate the suffering of people and nonhuman animals we might never meet. But we don't imagine the relevant feelings every time we make a purchase. I know I don't.

However, if we buy something we wouldn't have bought had we had fully and vividly imagined the felt consequences of doing so, then that purchase must be the product of an empathy-limiting mistake.

Another domain in which it can be very difficult to imagine the causal connection between our actions and someone else's suffering is when the action in question is the use of harmful language.

There are two main ways language can cause harm. The most obvious way is when someone hears your words and experiences pain, fear, or anger because of them. The causal link here isn't difficult to imagine; however, we often cause this kind of suffering due to a lack of knowledge (as we've already discussed).

The second way one's choice of language can cause harm is when the use of certain phrases contributes to or cements a way of thinking about a particular group of people. The harm here is less direct. It can be difficult for privileged folk to imagine the ways language structures thought and thereby action, but the people on the receiving end of harmful language and those actions don't have to imagine. They experience directly the many ways that words matter.

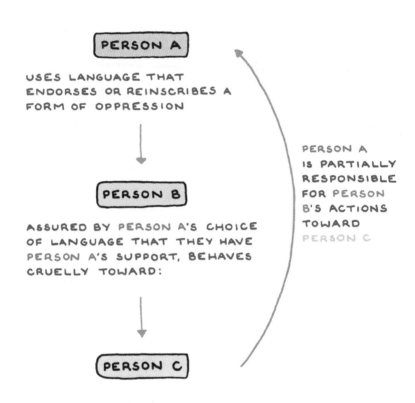

PERSON A

USES LANGUAGE THAT
ENDORSES OR REINSCRIBES A
FORM OF OPPRESSION

PERSON B

ASSURED BY PERSON A'S CHOICE
OF LANGUAGE THAT THEY HAVE
PERSON A'S SUPPORT, BEHAVES
CRUELLY TOWARD:

PERSON C

PERSON A
IS PARTIALLY
RESPONSIBLE
FOR PERSON
B'S ACTIONS
TOWARD
PERSON C

One example of this has been highlighted by many intersex activists.[19] To be intersex is to be born with a set of sex characteristics that don't line up with those that people tend to think of as typically "male" or typically "female." Language that pathologizes those features can shape the way people think about them. If we refer to the healthy variations an intersex person's body exhibits as a "disorder of sexual development" or as a sex trait that a man's body "shouldn't" have, we're introducing normative language where it doesn't belong.[20] These words contribute to the maintenance of a society in which those traits that distinguish intersex people are framed as medical problems in need of fixing. And this framing contributes to the marginalization and the unnecessary, potentially harmful surgeries intersex people face.[21]

We often fail to grasp why language matters as much as it does to oppressed groups we're not a part of. The connections between language and violent actions and structures are never as visible to people who don't suffer their harm. This is the type of mistake that results in privileged folk railing against political correctness, rather than recognizing how language can make them complicit in cruelty (I should know; I've been one of those people).

POLITICAL CORRECTNESS
HAS GONE TOO FAR

IS WHAT PRIVILEGED PEOPLE CALL IT
WHEN MEMBERS OF MARGINALIZED
COMMUNITIES ASK FOR BASIC RESPECT
FOR THEIR HUMANITY.

DUE TO THE ABSURDLY SELF-DEFEATING NATURE OF SUCH A FEAT, THE PHRASE "PULLING ONESELF UP BY THE BOOTSTRAPS" ORIGINALLY MEANT A TASK WAS IMPOSSIBLE.

HOW IRONIC, THEN, THAT IT NOW SERVES AS A MAXIM FOR THE IMPOVERISHED THROUGH WHICH RICH WHITE MEN SHIRK THEIR RESPONSIBILITY FOR HOARDING WEALTH.

Using harmful, inaccurate language is a bit like disposing of plastic in the ocean: If one person did it, it wouldn't be much of a problem—though we might think that one person was a bit of an oddball—but if a large group of people do it, and somehow assure one another that it's an OK thing to do, the ocean is screwed.

Which brings us nicely to our final example of empathy-limiting failures of imagination: our failure to imagine the results of contributing to ecological disaster.

Many of us are aware that our lifestyle decisions and political activity can affect the amount of CO_2 emitted going forward, and that only by drastically reducing the rate at which CO_2 is emitted can we avert the later stages of the current climate catastrophe. However, the feat of imagination that is required for that abstract knowledge to become empathetically motivated action is gargantuan.[22]

It's almost impossible to picture the connection between campaigning for better public transport provision and the harm caused by global heating; to do so we'd have to vividly call to mind how that campaigning might in some small way help to avert suffering brought about by widespread droughts, starvation, and the end of even more indigenous ways of life.

It's rare that we are motivated to act by pain to which we are so distantly connected. Climate change empathy is made trickier by the large time lag between the overexploitation of carbon-based fuels and the awful consequences of that greed, and the tendency for that exploitation to occur in wealthy nations while the consequences are experienced (initially, at least) in poorer ones—making the required exercise of imagination even less likely to occur. But when we act in a way that we wouldn't have if we had only imagined more fully or vividly the consequences of acting that way, that action represents an error.

SPATIAL
TEMPORAL
SOCIAL
+ CAUSAL DISTANCE ————————————→

EMPATHY LESS LIKELY
BUT NO LESS NEEDED

Failures of imagination can switch your empathy off. If you can be cruel only because you fail to imagine those who experience your cruelty, that cruelty is the product of an empathy-limiting mistake.

Limiting conceptions of morality can switch our empathy off

There's one final type of empathy-limiting mistake I'd like to outline, and it might be the trickiest group to get a handle on. I want to talk about those empathy-limiting mistakes we make when we're beholden to an unambitious or misdirected conception of our moral duties.

A large portion of human cruelty is, in fact, perpetrated in the name of morality, and many of our failures to be kind are born of a misplaced belief in the moral superfluousness of that particular kindness.

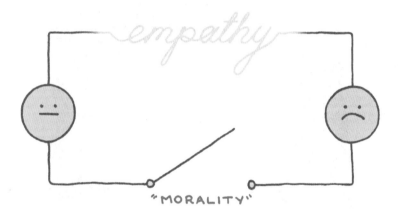

Earlier, I pointed out that many explanations besides empathy have been proposed to explain kindness. I tried to get across the importance of arriving at (what I take to be) the right explanation. And one of the reasons I believe it's so important to recognize empathy as the source of your kindness is that alternative explanations can turn your empathy off.

I CAN'T HELP IT. WHEN I'M BACKED INTO A CORNER, MY CLAWS COME OUT.

WHEN SOMEONE POINTS OUT THE WAYS IN WHICH YOU ARE COMPLICIT IN CRUELTY, YOU AREN'T BACKED INTO A CORNER; YOU'RE BEING OFFERED A CLEAR ROUTE FORWARD.

Let's look at the belief that the source of human kindness is rules and a fear that without them society would break down. If you believe rules are the source of your duty to be kind and abstain from cruelty, you will be kind only to the extent that the rules demand. You'll switch off your empathy when you have met that threshold.

HM, NOTHING ABOUT NOT BEING RACIST IN HERE.

Don't get me wrong—rules aren't universally bad. They can serve as useful guides for introducing our bare minimum, moral duties, and as a framework against which we can hold each other accountable. But they can be taken too seriously. Some people, for instance, think the often-useful rule "Tell the truth" is a basic tenet of morality. If those people were confronted with a distraught child who asked them why the family dog needed to move to the happy farm, they would think it their duty to respond, "Well, actually, your dog isn't on a farm at all. He was hit by a car and your parents are liars." This would clearly represent a failure to empathize with what the child was feeling.

Rules that have been mistaken for morality frequently lead us to act cruelly. Many people, for instance, mistake those rules of property and ownership upon which our capitalist system is built for moral rules, and they limit their empathy for that reason.

Believing that property rights aren't merely artificial constructs—morally justifiable only to the extent that they do more good than harm—but are the beginning and end of morality itself results in adherents of that belief seeing taxation and wealth redistribution as immoral. It tends to be wealthy folk, those with the most to gain, who want to grant the rules of a laissez-faire economy (and unsurprisingly, only those rules) this undeserved status as basic moral facts. Making this mistake switches off one's empathy toward those on the poverty end of a grossly unequal distribution of wealth.

Any morality based on an inflexible list of rules can stop its believers from empathizing. If you think our duties to one another take the form of a list of prohibitions—"Thou

SOLD
FOR AN AMOUNT THAT COULD HAVE FED THOUSANDS BUT IT'S OK BECAUSE NO RULES WERE BROKEN

shalt not x," "Thou shalt not y"—you will fail to recognize the need to attend to particular features of a situation. All the thinking has been done for you in advance, so you'll see no need to listen to and empathize with the people your actions affect; just follow the rules and you're above criticism and can silence guilt.

Rules that are currently switching people's empathy off include: marriage can only be between a man and a woman, charity begins at home, the Second Amendment, you must wear the clothes of the sex you were assigned at birth, and borders must only be crossed with permission.

Another type of rule that pops up a lot are those that draw an arbitrary distinction between action and inaction. Rule-based systems of morality often distinguish between not acting and thereby permitting harm to continue, and acting to bring about that very same harm. While the empathetic account of morality I've proposed would recognize equal culpability in either case, rules mostly prescribe what we mustn't do, and have little to say about what we must do.

✗ WE CANNOT BE BLAMED
   FOR NOT ACTING.

✓ INACTION IS A FORM OF
   ACTION AND WE ARE
   JUST AS RESPONSIBLE
   FOR ITS CONSEQUENCES.

Few rules demand that you do something actively cruel, but a rule-based moral code can let you off the hook for your inaction in the face of suffering. Many empathy-limiting moral systems simply set the bar for how much we owe one another too low. And in doing so, they grant us the opportunity to limit our empathy.

This final group of empathy-limiting mistakes can be the hardest to challenge. Widely accepted moral norms are often unshakable, but like all other beliefs, they can be wrong.

Through the institution of shared rules and practices, we convince ourselves and one another that particular types of kindness are too much to ask, and that certain forms of cruelty are permissible. Once these norms become fixed habits of thought, empathy never gets its chance to kick in and scream, "Fuck that!"

Mistakenly believing that we owe one another only circumscribed forms of assistance, or that causing suffering in particular ways can be justified on the basis of religion, law, or rationality, will stop you from acting as you would if your empathy weren't limited by those beliefs. The wrong "morality" can switch your empathy off.

You are kind because of empathy. You aren't kinder because of mistakes that have limited that empathy. If you recognized and corrected those mistakes, your empathy would expand. In this chapter, I've given some examples of common empathy-limiting mistakes broken down by type, a taxonomy of errors that might enable our cruelty. We looked at how false beliefs, a lack of knowledge, failures of imagination, and limiting conceptions of morality can all turn our empathy off.

Hopefully, now that we've looked at some examples of what commonly limits kindness, you're convinced that these are bad limits. In any other context, you wouldn't accept feeling a particular way due to a failure of knowledge or imagination; you'd see feelings based on straightforward mistakes like these as misplaced. The same is true of your empathy. You'll want to empathize as you would in the absence of these errors.

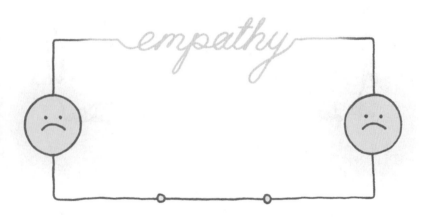

All that stands between us and radically kinder versions of ourselves are the empathy-limiting mistakes we haven't yet spotted. My hope is that you now have a map and the impetus for spotting and tackling these mistakes. Doing so will make you drastically kinder, or at least equip you to be so the next time you get the chance.

IF YOU ACT AS YOU'RE EXPECTED TO, YOU'RE LIKELY TO ENGAGE IN SOCIALLY ENCOURAGED FORMS OF CRUELTY.

●●●● 7 ●●●●

Exercising empathy

If I've done my job right, you're kinder now. But you'll want to stay kinder, and to keep getting kinder and kinder. Now that you've noticed mistakes were limiting your kindness, you'll want to locate and undermine all those mistakes that are still switching your empathy off, and to avoid making any new ones.

So what's next? How does one become less prone to ignorance-induced cruelty?

The answer is simple: We just have to listen. Listen to the people our actions affect, listen to people whose lives are very different from ours, and listen to those we've been discouraged from listening to.

If ignorance is empathy's poison, listening is the only known antidote.

Listening exercises our empathy muscles and challenges the ignorance that can enfeeble them. We must talk about how we can become better listeners, because good listening is—to butcher Leonard Cohen's words—where the empathy light gets in.

How to listen

The final question of this book is, how can one become a better listener?

If you're to continue getting kinder and kinder long after you've finished this book, it will be because it inspired you to listen more widely, to listen better, and to act on the empathy that your listening unleashes.

(I'm fortunate enough to have as my love-partner the best listener I've ever met. This whole book is inspired by her, but this chapter even more than the rest.)

Listening is a skill, and an underrated one at that. There's a tendency to view listening not as a skill but as a character trait, to associate that character trait with femininity, and to denigrate it or minimize its importance by that association.[1] Being a "good listener" is seen by many as womanly. It's seen as a nice thing to be but not important or powerful, like the "masculine" virtues of intellect and leadership.

But listening is a hard-won ability; getting good at it takes practice, and it can require exhausting mental effort to listen well. Listening isn't easy. Thinking some people are just better at it than others and nothing can be done about that is an excuse to avoid the hard work of good listening. The best listener I know wasn't born that way; she continually works at that skill because she values it so highly.[2]

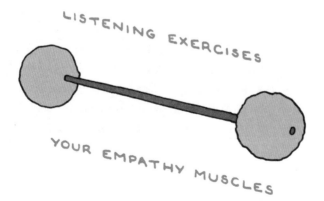

LISTENING EXERCISES

YOUR EMPATHY MUSCLES

Without the ability to listen, we would know life only from our own perspective; we'd never learn how it feels to be anyone but ourselves. And under the view of kindness and morality presented in this book, listening isn't some nice add-on to being a good person; it's the essential starting point. Through failing to listen, we cultivate the ignorance that limits our kindness. It is only by putting in the work of good listening that we can prevent empathy-limiting mistakes and reliably do the right thing.

Here are some tips for revolutionary, empathy-expanding listening.

◆ There are a million ways to listen; find the one that suits you.

By listening, I am not just referring to the act of hearing someone speak while they relay their experience. There are a million ways to listen. It can involve watching documentaries, movies, and YouTube videos; learning from podcasts, history shows, and the news; reading poetry, autobiographies, and essays; and chatting with people off-line and on social networks.

By listening, I mean any conscious effort we make to learn about and internalize someone else's experience. Find the type of listening that suits you, and listen in a way that gives you the greatest ability to take in what someone different from you is trying to tell you about their life and the lives of people like them.

DOING THE RIGHT THING
IN ONE DOMAIN DOESN'T
LET YOU OFF THE HOOK
IN ANY OF THE OTHERS.

◆ *Listen widely and directly; treat people as experts in themselves.*

Listen to everyone. Listen to those you live alongside every day (whom your actions are mostly likely to immediately affect), and to those whose lives are most incomparable to your own; listen to people all over the world and listen to the people on the furthest margins of your own society.

We must take care with whom we let filter or editorialize our listening, else we risk powerful people with ulterior motives thwarting our access to greater knowledge. Listen directly to those people whose lives you need to learn about, because they are the only ones with direct access to their own experience.

Remember that oppression forces you to become an expert on that oppression, and privilege fosters in you an obliviousness that is its parallel. If we want to learn about forms of oppression, we have to listen to their survivors directly.

I WANT TO LEARN ABOUT
THE HARMS OF
DEFORESTATION. WHOM
SHOULD I LEARN FROM?

• *Listen to those who are multiply oppressed.*

A mistake made over and over again by those aiming to learn about a particular form of oppression has been listening exclusively to those who are privileged in every other regard. Those who want to learn about oppression on the basis of gender often set about doing so by listening to wealthy cis white women; this will teach only a fraction of what we need to know and will frequently misdirect our empathy.

To avoid empathy-limiting mistakes toward Black women, for example, it's not enough to listen to Black men and white women and sum up what we learn. Black women's oppression cannot be understood by adding together the oppression that Black men and white women face. The oppression faced by Black women is greater than and different from the sum of its parts.[3] Moya Bailey, a scholar of critical race, feminist, and disability studies, and Trudy, an indie creator, writer, social critic, and womanist, coined and developed, respectively, the word *misogynoir* to describe this unique form of anti-Black misogyny.[4, 5]

In 1989, Kimberlé Crenshaw, a legal and critical race scholar, civil rights activist, and leading thinker in Black feminist legal theory, introduced the word *intersectionality* to describe perspectives on the interaction of multiple forms of oppression, which recognize that when axes of oppression are considered in isolation, the experiences of those people who exist where multiple axes intersect are obscured.[6]

When multiple axes of oppression combine, they create unique, compound forms. These intersectional oppressions must be studied in their own right, not pushed aside as unhelpful complications, or subsumed into a universalizing account.

They ought to be the central focus of any serious anti-oppression work.[7]

Our tendency in trying to listen more widely is to listen first—and exclusively—to those who are privileged in every way except one. So it's necessary that we make a concerted effort to do the precise opposite: We must center the experiences of those who are multiply oppressed.

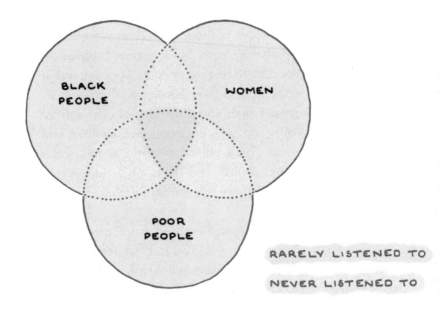

BLACK PEOPLE

WOMEN

POOR PEOPLE

RARELY LISTENED TO

NEVER LISTENED TO

• *Hear what's being said, not what you expect or want to hear.*

Whenever we listen to someone, we arrive with our own expectations of what it is they'll say. If we're not careful, these expec-

YES, SOME BIRDS DO IT,
AND SOME BEES DO IT,
BUT NO ONE OWES IT
TO YOU.

tations can stop us from listening to what they actually say. We have a tendency to mentally rehash what someone tells us, morphing their account into something that resembles the image of their experience that we arrived at the conversation with.

You need to work hard at listening with an open, flexible mind—not a mind ready to hear only what fits the current picture.

Often the current picture will be the one that presents you in the most favorable light, the one that hides the suffering of others from view, particularly when you are complicit in that suffering. This brings us to the next listening tip.

* *Avoid defensiveness at all costs.*

The most insurmountable barrier to listening is defensiveness.[8] When someone teaches us something about their experience that forces us to recognize the role we've played—through action or inaction—in their suffering, we have a tendency to shut down.

Informing people of the felt consequences of their actions, or how they could behave differently going forward to minimize the harm they cause, is not an attack, but many of us experience it as one.

In some instances, the empathy-limiting mistakes we learn about are ones that we've been making for as long as we can remember. When we find ourselves on the cusp of that realization, it's tempting to respond with fear, anger, or defensiveness. It can be tempting to try to fight back.

But attacking the messenger will never alter the truth of the message. Trying to defend ourselves against a painful realization is understandable but poisonous to moral growth. You cannot listen to and attack someone at the same time.

It is exactly in the areas in which learning something new makes you most uncomfortable and most painfully aware of your past actions that you have to listen closely. The stakes are too high; missing an opportunity to recognize your part in large-scale structures of cruelty just to protect an internal image of yourself as a good person is a risk too great to take.

◆ *So take your time and be present.*

Take a breath. Take a beat. When you're listening and you feel defensiveness welling up, sit with your thoughts for a moment.

In conversation, don't rush. Don't second-guess what your conversational partner is about to say; don't cut them off by trying to finish their sentences. Give them time and attention. Try to notice when your mind is elsewhere, and work on returning to the present. Ask questions that check your understanding and demonstrate your concern for getting it right.

When learning from books, videos, or podcasts, give new ideas the time they need to percolate. Don't rush to form settled, inflexible opinions. Be willing to be undecided and to keep listening to the voices that make you defensive.

We rarely change our minds the precise moment we are introduced to a new idea. I know that I never do. But if you don't shut down, and instead let what you've heard or read sit on your mental back burner for a while, that insight will often feel less threatening when you return to it; you may find you're suddenly able to acknowledge its truth.

Give new ideas the space they need. Give yourself time and space to learn.

◆ *Get comfortable being wrong, even drastically wrong.*

If we really want to learn about the world and our impact on it, we have to keep in mind the possibility discussed at the start of this book that we are not just sometimes a little bit unkind, but that we might in fact be a million miles the wrong side of moral.

Isn't it likely that, just like every generation before ours, many of us are currently perpetrating serious moral wrongs that we are (culpably) oblivious to? With that in mind, it's important that we get comfortable getting things wrong, even drastically wrong, and accepting that we have.

You might find, if you are particularly privileged, that while listening more broadly, you start to feel terrible about the sheer quantity of suffering and the many ways you are complicit in that suffering. You might be tempted to wallow in the shame of that realization, and the apathy and hopelessness that follows. But to do so is another manifestation of privilege. Only privileged folk have the option of noticing oppression and our part in it and freezing up in self-indulgent guilt. Get comfortable being uncomfortable and getting stuff done anyway.

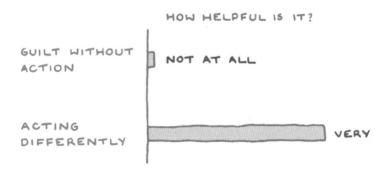

It's helpful, in my experience, to let go of the notion of "good" people and "bad" people. Many of us spend far too much time trying to reconcile the moral mistakes we've made with a belief that we are ultimately good. This self-assessment of our moral caliber is a distraction. The truth is there are not two distinct types, good people and bad people; we are all capable, under the right conditions, of serious cruelty and courageous kindness.

"Am I good or bad?" isn't the right question. Instead, ask yourself questions like: When did I last change my mind about something that matters? In what ways am I showing up to try to get things right? In what ways am I trying to learn so that I can do better and be better tomorrow?[9]

◆ *Get to know your privilege.*

Nothing gets hackles up like asking people to get to know their privilege, but it's crucial that we do so. One way we can learn about other people's lives is by recognizing the ways they're different from our own. Getting to know your privilege will help you notice advantages you benefit from that others don't, and barriers faced by some people but not by you.[10]

HUH, I HAD THE PRIVILEGE FILTER ON THIS WHOLE TIME.

Exploring your own privilege as a counterpoint—a photo negative—to another group's oppression will also help you to see the ways that privilege has developed in you certain kinds of ignorance. It's only by getting to know your privilege that you get familiar with those structures that have encouraged and incentivized you in your empathy-limiting mistakes. It's only by getting to know your privilege that you'll learn how you've benefited from the harm it's done to others.

◆ *Believe marginalized folk.*

Getting to know your privilege will show you why you're no expert on the forms of oppression you don't face; next, you need to believe the people who are when they tell you how those forms of oppression function.

When someone says, "Believe women!" they are not claiming that women, unlike people of other genders, are incapable of deceit. They are pointing to and suggesting we counter our society's tendency to do the precise opposite: to actively disbelieve women.

When you've been trained to disbelieve members of a particular group, making an active, conscious effort to do the opposite, to recognize that you have no good reason to interpret them as deceitful, can be revolutionary. Disbelief of the oppressed is a crucial piece in the armor of the current power structure. To believe members of an oppressed group is to challenge that which demands you disbelieve them.[11]

◆ *Create and hold space for people to be heard.*

You can listen only if there is someone willing to share their experience. But people usually share experiences only when they feel safe to do so (this isn't entirely true; there are a whole bunch of incredibly brave people who testify to their experi-

THE OTHER CUCUMBERS
ARE INSISTING THAT WE
ONLY LIVE LONGER DUE
TO THE DIFFERENT
ENVIRONMENT IN WHICH
WE GET TO EXIST.

WELL NOW WE'RE
REALLY IN A PICKLE.

ence despite it being far from safe to do so, but they shouldn't have to).

A part of good listening is contributing to and maintaining spaces in which the people you need to hear from feel that it's safe to speak.

Safety, in the sense relevant here, refers to the absence of risk of not only physical harm but also psychological and emotional harm. Sharing lived experiences, particularly painful ones, makes a person vulnerable to the many ways in which that act of courage can be disrespected. Dire harm is done to a person when they share their truth and are made to regret it. So if you want people to share their stories with you, you have to learn to treat those stories with the respect they deserve.

NO ONE I KNOW HAS EXPERIENCED SEXUAL VIOLENCE.

OR, NO ONE YOU KNOW HAS FELT SAFE ENOUGH TO DISCLOSE THAT EXPERIENCE TO YOU.

Creating and holding space on a personal, conversational level means demonstrating that you are capable of listening calmly, nonjudgmentally, attentively, and without trying to fix people's problems. It means showing your willingness to challenge your own internalized prejudices, so that you can hear what's truly being said.

From a broader perspective, we cannot read books, watch movies, and listen to podcasts made by people from oppressed groups if they are unable to produce them. Sometimes creating and holding space means paying for the work and the platforms that we need more of in this world. It means paying artists, poets, directors, and authors from marginalized communities so that they can keep telling their stories. Sometimes it can mean taking the platform you find yourself on and passing it to someone else, who can use it to tell a truth they're better placed to perceive.

◆ *Interpret charitably.*

In philosophy there is a concept called the principle of charity. It suggests that the best way to engage with what someone else is telling you is to interpret it in the strongest, most convincing form.

The opposite of the principle of charity is an argumentative strategy called straw-manning, in which you reconstruct the weakest possible version of a view you disagree with to make it easy to refute. To straw-man someone is the very opposite of listening, but it is often what we do when we find someone else's view uncomfortable to hear.

STRAW MAN

It's easy to critique; it's a lot harder to sincerely interpret others as having something important to say that we might learn from. But it's well worth the effort.

◆ *Concern yourself with content, not tone.*

Another barrier we face in listening is our tendency to disregard what someone is saying if we dislike their tone or manner of communication.

Often (for classist and/or racist reasons) we consider certain manners of speaking and ways of comporting oneself in conversation to convey some deficiency on the part of the speaker. If someone doesn't share our dialect or our cultural points of reference, or doesn't concern themselves with making us comfortable with what they're saying, we tend not to listen to them.

We also tend to switch off when someone is communicating while emotional. There's a common belief that if someone cannot contain their anger or their sadness while they are telling us

something, they can't be reliable, so we are justified in not listening.[12]

We often mistake emotion for irrationality, and a lack of emotion for rationality. We're more prone to listening to those who can make their point without crying, swearing, or shouting.

But again, this serves to cement power and privilege.[13] It will often be easier for a person with privilege to remain emotionless in a conversation with a person from an oppressed group about that oppression than vice versa. That's because the privileged person will usually have less at stake. If we listen only to those people who are not emotionally invested in what they're saying, we're likely to find ourselves listening only to the privileged.

WHAT'S AT STAKE IN A
CONVERSATION ABOUT
OPPRESSION?

FOR THOSE WHO ARE
PRIVILEGED

FOR THOSE WHO ARE
OPPRESSED

In its worst form, this focus on tone results in tone policing.[14] Tone policing labels a pattern whereby a member of a privileged group (particularly a white man) tells a member of an oppressed group (particularly a Black woman) that she would be more likely to convince him—or people like him—if she could just say it in a nicer, calmer, less angry way.

Tone policing is a tactic for derailing the true conversation at hand. But it also demands additional emotional labor from the member of the oppressed group, who is asked not just to communicate their experience but to suppress their understandable emotional response as they do so.

To be a good listener, you must work on your ability to hear people even when they're angry—in fact, particularly when they're angry. Do not let your desire to feel comfortable, your desire to not see someone in pain or enraged, get in the way of your ability to hear someone you need to hear.

◆ *Don't interrogate or demand trauma stories.*

I've said that you need to listen to the most oppressed and marginalized people because those are the people toward whom your empathy is most likely to be switched off. But please don't take that to mean you should interrogate the next disabled migrant woman you meet and demand she tell you of her worst trauma. That would very much be the wrong lesson to take from this book.

No one owes you their story; no one owes you an education on their oppression.

But there are people doing this work; there are people from marginalized groups who have already written books and made films, who are working as educators on these topics. Go to them (pay them if they're doing this work as paid employment, and recompense them however you can if they do it on a voluntary basis) and learn from them in whatever way they have chosen to teach. Don't take up space and demand answers. Take your time. Listen, let the ideas percolate, and learn.

Act

We've all got huge empathy reservoirs. The problem has been the plumbing. The pipes, bends, valves, taps, and cisterns have been rigged up using instructions that weren't fit for purpose. The empathetic capacity is there, but its flow has been redirected, limited, and blocked by our blunders.

When you practice good listening, it's like inviting a skilled plumber into your head. With everything you learn, the plumber replaces a dodgy pipe, unblocks the clogs of self-deceit, turns on the taps you've been quite comfortable keeping closed, and your empathy flows.

Sounds lovely, doesn't it? But the fact is, it won't always feel lovely. When our empathy toward someone has been turned off, it can feel like crap when it finally kicks in. It's not just that we've now got some new pain to partake in; it's the extra discomfort of acknowledging our failure to attend to that pain in the past, and our poor reasons for doing so.

I'm guessing you'll do the listening work anyway, in part because you want to do the right thing, and in part because you definitely don't want to do the wrong thing just because you were ignorant. I don't know anyone who'd be comfortable thinking they were acting a particular way only because of a mistake, and I'm hoping that this motive to get things right, to believe accurately, to see things as they really are is enough.

That motive, when combined with a recognition that we get a lot wrong when it comes to other people—in fact, we're set up to get things wrong when it comes to other people—will compel us to do the work of learning by listening, to make sure we're spotting and correcting those mistakes.

This book would all be for nothing, though, if you didn't act differently after you empathized differently. Kindness and morality aren't about feeling the right way; they're about how you act. I've approached the problem of making you kinder the way I have because I believe there's a necessary connection between unimpeded empathy and acting morally (I believe moral action just is that action you'd be motivated by empathy to pursue were that empathy not limited by mistakes). I find it impossible to believe people could act as they do if they were vividly aware of the hurt they were causing.

But often the acting will be even harder than the feeling. Changing your mind can be uncomfortable, but stepping up and acting can be costly in other ways.

There's a popular saying that kindness costs nothing. I get where it comes from; there are many forms of basic decency that are so straightforward as to make it unbelievable that people fail to perform them, like using the correct pronouns for someone, or giving up one's seat on a train to someone less able to stand.

But if we are only performing those acts of kindness that cost nothing, I'm afraid we're far from doing enough. Some-

times, doing the right thing will cost an awful lot, and it will still be the right thing. We set our standards far too low when we tell people that kindness costs nothing.

KINDNESS

~~COSTS NOTHING~~

CAN COST AN AWFUL
LOT AND STILL BE
REQUIRED OF YOU.

After all this listening, and all the repairs to your empathy plumbing that listening will bring about, you're going to spot more suffering, and you'll see just how much of it is avoidable. The larger part of suffering is human-made and is maintained as a result of shared, socially reinforced empathy-limiting mistakes.

That disgusts and angers me (and makes me ashamed of my role in maintaining those mistakes and that cruelty), and I imagine you feel the same way. But what are we going to do about it?

I said at the start that this isn't a book of practical, political advice; there'll be no list of kind acts to perform here. This book will make you kinder by strengthening your kindness motivation, not by telling you how to direct your preexisting motivation into action.

That's been my strategy largely because it's on the more meta questions that I think I might have something to add. It's also in the abstract that I think most people get lost; our thoughts on moral matters depart from one another's long before we've arrived at our specific disagreements about what actions we ought to start taking. These specific arguments are a symptom of a much deeper and broader discrepancy in our accounts of why, what, and how much we owe one another.

I've also refrained from providing practical next steps because writing of that kind already exists, and it's written far better than I would have managed. Google "How to be an ally to immigrants" and you'll be served millions of informative results, many written by those with lived expertise on the topic, replete with actions one could take.

The problem is, you can reliably predict which of your acquaintances would never seek out or act on such a list, and which might read it just to scoff. The game is usually won or lost long before we get to the point of practical tips. That's why we went further back—we had to do some of the meta-kindness work. This book and the empathy clogs it unblocks will, I hope, spur every reader to turn up to each practical request for moral action readier to do the right thing.

But we still have to actually do the right thing. Empathy must become action. And the final (hitherto unmentioned) barrier to that action is all the countervailing emotions and desires we have. Far from costing nothing, doing the right thing may well cost a lot. Once you've unleashed your empathy, you'll at some point find yourself empathetically motivated to take actions that cost you friendships, opportunities, wealth, status, and safety.

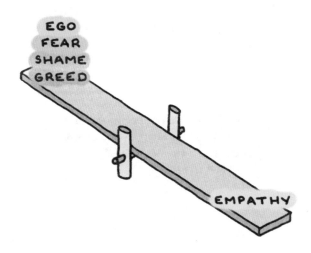

Your empathy, once unbounded, will demand that you act to sacrifice your comfort to avert someone else's agony, it will require that you uncomfortably call out friends who speak cruelly from their own place of empathetic parochialism, and it will push you to give up and redistribute that power that ought never have been yours to begin with. There will be many occasions when your mind will host a tug-of-war between your empathy and some other motive—maybe your desire for success, tasty food, or a pleasing self-image.

(Again, I'm not claiming empathy always wins out in me; this book isn't written from a place of kindness superiority.)

You may even meet people who tell you that your empathy is a weakness, or that you empathize too much; they'll tell you that experiencing too strongly the feelings of others will hold you back. They'll call you sentimental and soft because your rejection of empathy-limiting self-deceit will make them uncomfortable. Your defection from mutually assured ignorance will strike them as an affront, like a spotlight on their own failures to empathize.

ANYONE WHO IS KIND IN WAYS I'M NOT WILLING TO BE IS VIRTUE SIGNALING.

❋ ❋ ❋

All this is to say that I can't tell you which will win out: your unleashed empathy, or everything that pushes you to put the pipes back the way they were.

But this I do believe (to paraphrase a well-worn slogan): If empathy doesn't impel you to radical, disruptive kindness, you're not paying attention. If you aren't currently finding that even in the face of huge personal sacrifice empathy forces you to act, and to act in ways that go far beyond what people accept as reasonable kindness, I can't help but think that you're still making some empathy-limiting mistakes.

Conclusion

Picture if you will a parallel universe identical to this one in every way, except in this universe there exists a different version of you.

This alternate you is very much like you, but they have somehow managed to talk to every single person with whom we share this planet; they've spent some time listening to them and learning about their lives—their hopes, dreams, fears, and challenges.

And other-you is also incredibly knowledgeable about the world and the economic, political, social, and environmental systems that amplify the consequences of human action. This you is unmatched in their ability to imaginatively predict the future, as it will be influenced by what they do. They can vividly picture the distant consequences of every choice they consider, and can see in their mind's eye how everyone is likely to feel as a result. And they're incapable of obscuring their predictions through self-deceit. On top of all that, this version of you is entirely disabused of every human-made moral construct.

Imagine this you. Imagine how they might feel and act.

I contend that they'd be far kinder than you currently are (I'm not picking on you; the same would be true of the parallel, near-omniscient me). In fact, I reckon alternate-you would strike most people as radically, unreasonably kind. They'd be difficult and disruptive, constantly challenging the fucked-up way things are, and they'd be soft and gentle, willing to give so much of themselves to make those who are vulnerable feel safe and held.

They'd be this way because they wouldn't be able to help it. All that knowledge would leave them incapable of stifling their empathy. It'd be like all the taps were turned fully open and the handles had been broken off. Alternate-you would empathize with everyone who's capable of feeling anything, and would know exactly how to proceed on the basis of all that empathy.

All that separates you from this other version of you are mistakes. Other-you knows things that you don't, doesn't hold the false beliefs you do, and can imagine the consequences of your actions far better than you can. They are just you wholly absent any empathy-limiting ignorance. And in each instance that they'd act differently than you, they're acting as you would if you'd learned just a little more.

YOU

THINGS YOU HAVEN'T YET LEARNED

MUCH KINDER
YOU

Sadly, it's impossible for any of us to experience what this imagined duplicate has. None of us will have time to talk to everyone or to learn all there is to know about the planet we call home, and we'll all keep making some empathy-limiting mistakes for that reason. But we can all become less empathy-limited versions of ourselves.

There are already people doing the work of pointing out the many ways in which you depart from your full empathetic possibility. There are people—and their books, speeches, films, and essays—ready to correct the many mistakes currently enabling your departures from kindness. You just have to listen to them (this book will have comprehensively failed if the next one you pick up is also by a highly privileged cis white man).

I wrote this book to make you kinder. I've gone about it in the weird meta way I have because I'm a philosophy nerd. Personally, I just don't get those people who never lie awake at night, sweating beads of existential dread, tumbling through rabbit holes of progressively more abstract moral questions (if you're one of them, please teach me your ways); I don't get how one could stop these questions from becoming the primary, debilitating focus of one's life.

I hope I've convinced you that the most abstract moral questions and our answers to them matter. It would be exciting if I've managed only that, but I won't really be satisfied unless I've achieved the titular goal by convincing you of the strength of the answers given here.

Presented in this book is an account of what morality is,

why we're motivated to be (somewhat) moral, what limits our morality, and how and why we could be considerably better. It is just one account; you may well not like it or find it at all convincing (I know already that lots of philosophers won't, and they're going to be pissed at me for not doing justice in presenting any of the alternatives).

I've argued that moral facts (when properly understood) are facts about what your empathy would motivate you to do if you were making no mistakes that affected that empathy. I've also argued that we all have a tendency to make those mistakes, and that when it comes to the corrupting influence of power, we're actively encouraged to make them.

MORALITY

=

WHAT EMPATHY WOULD MOTIVATE
YOU TO DO IF YOU WERE MAKING
NO MISTAKES THAT AFFECTED
YOUR EMPATHY

This account of morality strikes me as true because the pull toward kindness—for me, at least—is the pull of empathy. When I've changed my mind on some moral question, it's always been because I've changed my mind on a related matter of fact, or paid attention to, or more vividly imagined some detail I'd been avoiding, which has unleashed previously unfelt empathetic concern (this change has always been the result of someone else being willing to do the work of educating me).

If, with a little extra information, I could be motivated by empathy to act completely differently than how I'm currently acting, I'm acting immorally. If someone's trying or has tried to give me that information and I won't listen because I don't want to act any differently, I'm culpable for acting immorally.

Over the past couple of years, I've had so many of these realizations, and they just keep coming. I'm working on being a better friend, son, and brother, a kinder stranger and shopper. I recognize the need to be active in the work of anti- racism, ableism, ageism, sexism, colonialism, and capitalism, transphobia, fatphobia, homophobia, and any other form of domination. I'm not yet satisfied with my efforts, and I don't know that I ever will be.

Say I've convinced you that fundamentally this is what morality is. To get you acting kinder I'll need to have also convinced you that you're making mistakes of this kind—that you're currently cruel in ways of which you've been willfully oblivious.

One fear—among many—I have about releasing this book into the wild is that one day a reader (if I'm lucky enough to have any) will say to me, "Wow, your book is such a good explanation of why everyone else behaves so badly." I worry that people could find this a compelling account of morality but fail to apply any of it in reflecting on their own behavior. My aim is to help each of us spot our own capacity for cruelty, but I expect we're more comfortable exploring all moral failings but our own. I really don't want to meet anyone—particularly anyone who holds a bunch of privilege—who thinks that this is a book about everyone but them; that form of complacency is how we keep getting back here.

This is a book about you because you're the one who picked it up. You could be considerably kinder: You could be someone

I WORSHIP THE
SUN BY FOLLOWING
HER WITH MY HEAD.

I WORSHIP HER
DIFFERENTLY BUT
DON'T FEEL
THREATENED BY
THAT DIFFERENCE.

who fucks shit up in the name of justice, and someone who those who constantly feel unsafe, feel safe around.

THIS IS A BOOK ABOUT YOU.

YOU COULD BE AND SHOULD BE MUCH, MUCH KINDER.

I've claimed that you and I are unlikely to be as kind or as moral as we ought to be because the threshold for "kind enough" was set far too low (like the temperature in an apartment where the landlord controls the thermostat).

How, then, will we know when we're truly offering the kindness we owe? There's no easy answer, but it will involve making sacrifices; we're certainly not doing enough if we're not giving anything up. Crucially, those of us with power must be willing to redistribute that power, because inequalities of power are inherently cruel, enable cruelty, and are largely what got us in this empathy-limiting mess in the first place.

We must act like the moral failings of our society represent a state of emergency, because they absolutely do.

You have a superpower and it's called empathy. But as Peter Parker's uncle recognized, with great power comes great responsibility. Your empathy is currently being switched off. If you don't do the work of good listening, of paying attention, you'll continue to be cruel in ways you otherwise couldn't and will fail to be outrageously kind in ways you otherwise would.

Much as the existence of this one-hundred-and-seventy-nine-page tome would suggest otherwise, kindness isn't a complicated matter; in the end it comes down to whether you choose to look or to look away. I hope this book has made it harder for you to choose the latter.

AN APPLE A DAY
KEEPS THE
DOCTOR AWAY.

SO DOES AN UNJUST
HEALTH CARE
SYSTEM IN WHICH
TIMELY MEDICAL
ATTENTION IS
RESERVED FOR THE
WEALTHY.

●●●● What to Read Next ●●●●

C learly this book has failed if you think of it as anything other than a starting point. Your next move, I hope, will be to read, listen to, or watch something made by someone you wouldn't normally make the effort to learn from. The larger part of my own reading has actually been done online. Below are some of the people who've taught me; this book would look completely different without them. Follow them on Instagram (or whatever you use) and you may come to feel as I do: grateful for the opportunities they've given me to be a little bit less shit. These are just some of my favorites; there are a million other educational socials to follow. Start with these and branch outward:

Anshika Khullar
(*Aorists*)

Alexandra Billings
(*TheRealAlexandraBillings*)

Charlie Craggs
(*Charlie_Craggs*)

Rachel Elizabeth Cargle (*Rachel. Cargle*)

Mona Chalabi (*MonaChalabi*)

Travis Alabanza
(*TravisAlabanza*)

Gina Martin (*GinaMartin*)

Munroe Bergdorf
(*MunroeBergdorf*)

Ericka Hart
(*IHartEricka*)

Sandy Ho
(*NotYourAvgHo*)

Chella Man (*ChellaMan*)

Thomas Page McBee (*ThomasPageMcBee*)

Florence Given (*FlorenceGiven*)

Paris Lees (*Paris.Lees*)

Ashton Attzs (*Attzs_*)

Kate Moross (*KateMoross*)

Shelby Lorman (*AwardsForGoodBoys*)

Char Ellesse (*EllesseChar*)

Sofie Hagen (*SofieHagenDk*)

Kuchenga (*Kuchenga*)

Suhaiymah Manzoor-Khan (*TheBrownHijabi*)

Tanya Compas (*TanyaCompas*)

Liv Little (*LivsLittle*)

Ketch Wehr (KetchWehr)

Sarah Day (SarahDayArts)

No White Saviors (*NoWhiteSaviors*)

Wednesday Holmes (*HelloMyNameIsWednesday*)

Hannah Daisy (*MakeDaisyChains*)

Jamie Windust (*Jamie_Windust*)

Ruth Finn Leiser (*Roobs_Grlclb*)

Megan Jayne Crabbe (*BodyPosiPanda*)

Fox Fisher (*TheFoxFisher*)

Natalie Byrne (*NatalieByrne*)

Tazia Cira (*TaziaCira*)

Lady Phyll (*LadyPhyll*)

Hazel Mead (*Hazel.Mead*)

Ashley C. Ford (*SmashFizzle*)

Ashley Lukashevsky (*AshLukaDraws*)

Aja Barber (*AjaBarber*)

Paula Akpan (*PaulaAkpan*)

Ben Hurst (*TheRealBenHurst*)

Shay-Akil McLean (*Hood_Biologist*)

Susannah Temko (*XYSuz*)

Trace Lysette (*TraceLysette*)

Layla F. Saad (*LaylaFSaad*)

Mia Mingus (*Mia.Mingus*)

Your Fat Friend (*YrFatFriend*)

Alok Vaid-Menon (*AlokVMenon*)

Scottee (*ScotteeIsFat*)

Nikesh Shukla (*NikeshShuklaWriter*)

Yves Mathieu (*The_YvesDropper*)

Gal-dem (*galdemzine*)

Owl (*UglaStefania*)

Pidgeon Pagonis (*pidgeo_n*)

And here is a list of things you might consider reading next (along with following up on some of the people in the Notes). It's an imperfect list, written from my imperfect knowledge. But if you engage with any of them, your empathy will expand a little. Then find out whom these people learned from and who cites them as teachers, and listen to what those people have to say too.

Sister Outsider, Audre Lorde

Zami: A New Spelling of My Name, Audre Lorde

About Us: Essays from the Disability Series of the New York Times, edited by Peter Catapano and Rosemarie Garland-Thomson

To My Trans Sisters, Charlie Craggs

Ain't I a Woman, bell hooks

Natives: Race and Class in the Ruins of Empire, Akala

The Good Immigrant (US and UK editions), edited by Nikesh Shukla and Chimene Suleyman

It's Not About the Burqa: Muslim Women on Faith, Feminism, Sexuality and Race, edited by Mariam Khan

Happy Fat: Taking Up Space in a World That Wants to Shrink You, Sofie Hagen

Queer: A Graphic History, Meg-John Barker and Jules Scheele

So You Want to Talk About Race, Ijeoma Oluo

Why I'm No Longer Talking to White People About Race, Reni Eddo-Lodge

What We Talk About When We Talk About Rape, Sohaila Abdulali

Hunger, Roxane Gay

Bad Feminist, Roxane Gay

Not That Bad, edited by Roxane Gay

Don't Touch My Hair, Emma Dabiri

Everyday Sexism, Laura Bates

Feminism Without Borders, Chandra Talpade Mohanty

Burgerz, Travis Alabanza

Wide Sargasso Sea, Jean Rhys

Freedom Is a Constant Struggle: Ferguson, Palestine, and the Foundations of a Movement, Angela Y. Davis

Whipping Girl, Julia Serano

Killing the Black Body, Dorothy Roberts

Revolting Prostitutes: The Fight for Sex Workers' Rights, Molly Smith and Juno Mac

Beloved, Toni Morrison

Amateur, Thomas Page McBee

Between the World and Me, Ta-Nehisi Coates

Care Work: Dreaming Disability Justice, Leah Lakshmi Piepzna-Samarasinha

The Fire Next Time, James Baldwin

Hostile Environment: How Immigrants Became Scapegoats, Maya Goodfellow

●●●● Acknowledgments ●●●●

The first acknowledgment must go to the role privilege and luck played in putting me in a position to write this book. Life is a rigged game and I was dealt an unfairly good hand, and that starting hand continues to make my life easier and safer, and provides me with opportunities from which others are excluded.

Next, I would like to acknowledge and thank those people who have believed in me along the way. I have a fragile ego that oscillates between "You have something super vital to add" and "You should never write or draw anything again, you loser." Sadly, I spend most of my time in the latter camp. That I got here owes a lot to people who have backed me, from my schoolteachers to my first hundred followers. The fact that Laura Macdougall took a chance on me, and has shown up in my corner with the gentleness I need ever since, has meant the world to me.

My Instagram friends must appear here. I want to knock on each of your doors and give you chocolate (or whatever snack you enjoy) and all the gratitude that's welling up in my eyes as I think of the role of our community, and all of you who've taught me so much about the way you experience this world's injustices. Thanking Instagram pals might seem corny and millennial, but honestly, you all made this happen. We form little communities of love, friendship, and reflection on there and beautiful things emerge. Everyone who has chatted to me or followed along online has kept me going long enough to make this.

Unending thanks must go to Shannon Kelly, Meg Leder, Amy Sun, Kym Surridge, Nayon Cho, Matt Giarratano, Carlynn Chironna, Fabiana Van Arsdell, Sabrina Bowers, Rebecca Gray, and everyone at Penguin and Profile who has had a hand in this, who believed in me and used their expertise, their insight, and the kindest of soft touches to make this the best book it could be.

Mum, Dad, Granny, Fred, Hollie, and Charlie—what a fucking team. I am proud of you individually and I am proud of us as a unit. We know about the hard-fought-for opportunities, the dinner table conversations, and the (sometimes stressful) you-can-do-anything-you-put-your-mind-to upbringing that forged us kids. I carry a part of each of you in everything I do. I am so proud of who my siblings have become, and the standards we hold each other to. I am so lucky to have this family team.

I'm also grateful to have added more family in Annet and Tania, who welcomed me with open hearts and whose love for the family unit is inspiringly fierce. Badass, empathetic single mothers produce badass, empathetic daughters who change the world—the Gardner family motto.

My BLVD friends: soft, kind, thoughtful humans; without finding and backing one another, would we have kept valuing these qualities?

Sam Toft, Kitty and I were outrageously lucky to move to Brighton and bump into the perfect (incredibly talented artist) friend. In you we've found inspiration and endless kindness.

Rachel Wilkerson Miller writes, "Behind every woke man is an exhausted feminist you need to thank." And people have applied the same insight to other forms of oppression. My biggest thanks, and yours if you liked this book, must go to my exhausted teachers. Many of them appear here, and in the Notes and What to Read Next section.

My most influential teachers, though, have been Kitty and the women she has introduced me to. Thanks to Kitty vouching for me, these women have invited me into a world of loving intimacy and sisterhood with a trust that I aspire to be worthy of. These women treat one another the way I dream we'll all treat one another someday. Katie, Sadie, Sonia, Elaine, Keely, Lena, Nina, Cynthia, and the women of Survivors' Network and Rise, thank you for what you've taught me: the power of soft strength channeled through hard feminist theory. Particular thanks to Elaine, Sadie, Katie, Stacey, and Julia, who offered insights and some key readings.

Kitty, words fail me, but I'll write some anyway (because I know how you love them). You are the kindest, bravest, smartest, strongest, funniest, cutest, and most thoughtful, reflective, beautiful, and inspiring being this universe ever expressed itself through. Your stubborn, seemingly naive belief in the best of people, while confronted with their worst, is the most impressive fuck-you to cruelty I've witnessed. Living and learning with you, and building a microcosmic utopia from which we draw the strength to build the macro one, is the greatest honor of my life.

When I think about our love, I think about the permission

we give each other: the permission to take off armor, to dream and realize preposterous dreams, to play with gender boxes, to be our whole selves, and to love those selves wholly in our love for each other. You are my best friend (thanks for making it romantical).

Love (romantic or in any of its other beautiful, intimate forms) is the source of our revolutionary power. It's through loving and being loved by some that we can learn to love all, and find the courage to create a society that channels that love.

Some of you know that Kitty proposed not-marriage to me in 2017—we won't be getting married but we want to have a love party and celebrate our ongoing mutual, consensual, anti-patriarchal commitment to each other with our loved ones someday (the plan is to do it beneath the tree in which we'll build our tree house). Anyway, I want an opportunity to propose not-marriage to her too. I'm using this book because I said Kitty's name should have been alongside mine on the front, but she disagreed. So instead, her name will appear at the end: I love you and I like you; will you be my best friend forever, Kitty Gardner?

Introduction

1. While this book addresses the same subject matter as moral philosophy (and particularly metaethics), I've made the conscious choice to sacrifice some academic rigor—and a whole lot of jargon—in the name of accessibility to a wider audience. One way this manifests is in my use, predominantly, of "kindness" language (rather than "moral" language). I have also made the decision to collapse the distinctions between the descriptive, normative, and semantic/metaethical interpretations of the question "What is morality?" For the purposes of this book, I think that's proved a worthy sacrifice. However, this book would not serve as a good introduction to academic metaethics. If you'd like to learn more about the landscape of that discipline (you should; it's fascinating), I'd suggest reading:

   Stephen Darwall, Allan Gibbard, and Peter Railton, "Toward Fin de Siecle Ethics: Some Trends," *Philosophical Review* 101, no. 1 (1992): 115–89.

   Geoff Sayre-McCord, "Metaethics," *The Stanford Encyclopedia of Philosophy*, ed. Edward N. Zalta (Stanford, CA: Metaphysics Research Lab, Stanford University, Summer 2014), https://plato.stanford.edu/archives/sum2014/entries/metaethics/.

2. Philosophers who have also given empathy a central place in their metaethical theses include David Hume, Adam Smith, Michael Slote, and Neil Sinhababu. The metaethical part of this book probably owes its biggest intellectual debt to Hume. It's worth noting, however, particularly because I never learned it during my time at university, that Hume was a white supremacist whose views on the inferiority of nonwhite people (conveyed in a footnote in David Hume, "Of National Characters," *The Philosophical*

Works of David Hume, vol. 3 [Edinburgh, Scotland: Adam Black and William Tait, 1826], 224–44) were employed in defense of slavery. I know this only thanks to the work of Shay-Akil McLean (@ hood_biologist).

3. I have included a What to Read Next section that lists many books like this, books that speak to the concrete and the particular far more than this one.

4. Something important to name from the get-go, because people often express the opposite view when talking about empathy: Autistic people do not lack empathy. You may not have thought otherwise, but if you did it's important that you're dissuaded from that myth before we really get going. Something crucial that's going on in that particular discussion is a distinction between emotional empathy and cognitive empathy. Emotional empathy is the vicarious experience of an emotional state perceived in another agent. In this book, I'm using the word *empathy* to refer only to emotional empathy (this is the type I take to be central in our motivation to be kind). Cognitive empathy, sometimes also called perspective-taking, is the process of imagining, or predicting, what someone else is thinking or feeling. A consensus seems to be forming that while autistic people may have a different capacity for perspective-taking (when measured in and against a neurotypical world), they have no less capacity for emotional empathy, and may in fact have more than neurotypical folk. Many autistic activists describe themselves as hyper empathetic (in the emotional sense), often finding themselves overwhelmed by an influx of other people's feelings. When it comes to cognitive empathy, the question is far from settled; many autistic activists and academics point out that perspective-taking is a two-way street, and that it's clear that neurotypical folk struggle to cognitively empathize with autistic folk at least as much as vice versa.

Read Lydia X. Z. Brown (Autistic Hoya) and Alaina Leary for autistic people describing their experiences of empathy:

Lydia X. Z. Brown, "Why Do I Think I'm Autistic…" *Autistic Hoya* (blog), December 12, 2015, https://www.autistichoya.com/2015/12/why-do-i-think-im-autistic.html.

Alaina Leary, "What It Means to Be Highly Empathetic, and Autistic," Medium, April 3, 2017, http://medium.com/the-establishment/what-it-means-to-be-highly-empathetic-and-autistic-e3cc3a05ebe6.

Damian Milton introduced the concept of the double empathy

problem to capture the possibility of seeing the perspective-taking challenges associated with autism as a two-way street: Damian E. M. Milton, "On the Ontological Status of Autism: The 'Double Empathy Problem,'" *Disability & Society* 27, no. 6 (2012): 883–7.

5. From Barack Obama's University of Massachusetts at Boston commencement address in 2006, "The biggest deficit that we have in our society and in the world right now is an empathy deficit."

6. "Oppressors always expect the oppressed to extend to them the understanding so lacking in themselves." From: Audre Lorde, *Sister Outsider* (New York: Crossing Press, 2007): 63.

1 • Why ask, "Why are we kind?"

1. Again, this would not be a good starting point if you wanted metaethics or normative ethics 101 (and I'm mixing in descriptive accounts of morality as well). This list isn't a fair representation of the strength of many of the alternative theories in those disciplines. Some people who present alternative theories I've found compelling include: Christine Korsgaard, Sharon Street, Michael Smith, Peter Railton, John Rawls, and Neil Sinhababu.

2 • We are kind because of empathy

1. For the empathy science, I have largely relied on the work of Stephanie Preston and Frans de Waal. See: Stephanie Preston and Frans de Waal, "Empathy: Its Ultimate and Proximate Bases," *Behavioral and Brain Sciences* 25, no. 1 (2002): 1–20; and Frans de Waal, "Putting the Altruism Back into Altruism: The Evolution of Empathy," *Annual Review of Psychology* 59 (2008): 279–300. And for a more accessible read: Frans de Waal, *The Age of Empathy: Nature's Lessons for a Kinder Society* (London: Souvenir Press, 2011). I have also found the work of Tania Singer, Jean Decety, Daniel Batson, and Jamil Zaki invaluable. All would be good starting points for your own research on the science of empathy.

2. This is the Humean theory of practical rationality and is contested, but well defended, in philosophy. See: Neil Sinhababu, "The Humean Theory of Practical Irrationality," *Journal of Ethics and Social Philosophy* 1 no. 6 (2011): 1–13.

3. Many philosophers would disagree here, particularly Immanuel Kant and his intellectual descendants, who reject the Humean

theory of practical rationality. Research that and moral rationalism broadly to head down a rabbit hole and learn some more on this.

3 · Empathy evolved

1. Inbal Ben-Ami Bartal, Jean Decety, and Peggy Mason, "Empathy and Pro-social Behavior in Rats," *Science* 334, no. 6061 (2011): 1427–30.

2. Mylene Quervel-Chaumette, Viola Faerber, Tamás Faragó, Sarah Marshall-Pescini, and Friederike Range, "Investigating Empathy-Like Responding to Conspecifics' Distress in Pet Dogs," *PloS One* 11, no. 4 (2016): e0152920.

3. Jules H. Masserman, Stanley Wechkin, and William Terris, " 'Altruistic' Behavior in Rhesus Monkeys," *American Journal of Psychiatry* 121, no. 6 (1964): 584–5.

4. "empathy evolved in animals as the main proximate mechanism for directed altruism, and… it causes altruism to be dispensed in accordance with predictions from kin selection and reciprocal altruism theory." From: de Waal, "Putting the Altruism Back into Altruism."

5. William D. Hamilton, "The Genetical Evolution of Social Behaviour. Parts I, II," *Journal of Theoretical Biology* 7 (1964): 1–52.

6. Robert L. Trivers, "The Evolution of Reciprocal Altruism," *Quarterly Review of Biology* 46, no. 1 (1971): 35–57.

7. Robert Axelrod and William D. Hamilton, "The Evolution of Cooperation," *Science* 211, no. 4489 (1981): 1390–6.

8. Frans de Waal refers to this as "veneer theory" in: Frans B. M. de Waal, "Morality and the Social Instincts: Continuity with the Other Primates," The Tanner Lectures on Human Values (lecture, Princeton University, Princeton, NJ, November 19–20, 2003).

9. I really wanted to go into the illuminating distinction between ultimate and proximate causes here, as it's important to keep in mind when explaining the presence of any naturally selected feature of an organism. The distinction was introduced in: Ernst Mayr, "Cause and Effect in Biology," *Science* 134, no. 3489 (1961): 1501–6.

10. François Jacob, "Evolution and Tinkering," *Science* 196, no. 4295 (1977): 1161–6.

11. Inbal Ben-Ami Bartal, David A. Rodgers, Maria Sol Bernardez

Sarria, Jean Decety, and Peggy Mason, "Pro-social Behavior in Rats Is Modulated by Social Experience," *eLife* 3 (2014): e01385.

4 Empathy has an off switch

1. The move I'm making here is inspired by ideal observer theories, particularly those espoused in: Roderick Firth, "Ethical Absolutism and the Ideal Observer," *Philosophy and Phenomenological Research* 12, no. 3 (1952): 317–45; and Peter Railton, "Moral Realism," *Philosophical Review* 95, no. 2 (1986): 163–207.

2. I have phrased these as rhetorical questions, but the answer to all is a resounding yes. Prejudice toward the out-group is reduced by contact with its members, and empathy has been shown to mediate this effect in meta-analysis: Thomas F. Pettigrew and Linda R. Tropp, "How Does Intergroup Contact Reduce Prejudice? Meta-analytic Tests of Three Mediators," *European Journal of Social Psychology* 38, no. 6 (2008): 922–34.

5 • The unequal distribution of empathy-limiting mistakes

1. The broad claim of this chapter, that inequalities of power affect knowledge acquisition—developing in the oppressed an expertise in their own oppression, and in the privileged a mirror ignorance—appears so frequently in and is so central to discussions of social justice that it's been hard to choose whom to cite. This epistemological turn (epistemology is the study of how we come to "know") has occurred in the study of most forms of oppression and their intersections. Some writings that have taught me about this include:

> bell hooks, *Feminist Theory: From Margin to Center* (Boston: South End Press, 1984).
> Patricia Hill Collins, "The Social Construction of Black Feminist Thought," *Signs: Journal of Women in Culture and Society* 14, no. 4 (1989): 745–73.
> Bat-Ami Bar On, "Marginality and Epistemic Privilege," in *Feminist Epistemologies*, ed. Linda Alcoff and Elizabeth Potter (New York: Routledge, 1993): 83–100.
> Charles W. Mills, "White Ignorance," in *Race and Epistemologies*

    of Ignorance, ed. Shannon Sullivan and Nancy Tuana (Albany: State University of New York Press, 2007), 11–38. Kristie Dotson, "Tracking Epistemic Violence, Tracking Practices of Silencing," *Hypatia* 26, no. 2 (2011): 236–57.

2. "... this cultural knowledge is most often inaccessible to white people, and when confronted with it, most white people are incredulous." From: Elijah Anderson, "This Is What It Feels Like to Be Black in White Spaces," *Guardian*, June 9, 2018, http://www.theguardian.com/commentisfree/2018/jun/09/everyday-racism-america-black-white-spaces.

3. Aimi Hamraie, "Designing Collective Access: A Feminist Disability Theory of Universal Design," *Disability Studies Quarterly* 33, no. 4 (2013).

4. Tressie McMillan Cottom, for example, writes of "knowing [her] whites," describing an ability learned out of necessity to "anticipate white people's emotions and fears and grievances because their issues are singularly our problem." From: Tressie McMillan Cottom, *Thick: And Other Essays* (New York: New Press, 2018), 98–126.

5. Pamela Pansardi, "Power to and Power over: Two Distinct Concepts of Power?" *Journal of Political Power* 5, no. 1 (2012): 73–89.

6. Here's one of those: Audre Lorde, *Zami: A New Spelling of My Name* (London: Sheba Feminist, 1984).

7. Here's one of those: Lorelei Lee, "Cash/Consent," *n+1*, Fall 2019, http://nplusonemag.com/issue-35/essays/cashconsent.

8. Here's one of those: Rachel McKinnon, "Stereotype Threat and Attributional Ambiguity for Trans Women," *Hypatia* 29, no. 4 (2014): 857–72.

9. Peggy McIntosh, "White Privilege: Unpacking the Invisible Knapsack," *Peace and Freedom*, July/August 1989.

10. This is related to the understanding of racism as prejudice *plus* power (prejudice not backed up by structural power isn't racism and cannot do anywhere near as much harm). Discussed in: Ijeoma Oluo, *So You Want to Talk About Race* (Berkeley, CA: Seal Press, 2018).

11. Rachel Elizabeth Cargle discusses this phenomenon more broadly on her incredibly educational Instagram platform (@rachel.cargle) and in: Rachel Elizabeth Cargle, "When Feminism Is White Supremacy in Heels," *Harper's Bazaar*, August 16, 2018, http://www.harpersbazaar.com/culture/politics/a22717725/what-is-toxic-white-feminism.

12. "... the election-year demand for empathy toward Trump support-
ers obscured the consequences of Trump's support for his targets."
From: Jamelle Bouie, "There's No Such Thing as a Good Trump
Voter," *Slate*, November 15, 2016, http://slate.com/news-and-
politics/2016/11/there-is-no-such-thing-as-a-good-trump-voter.
html.

6 · Mistakes that can turn empathy off

1. Laura Bates, *Everyday Sexism* (London: Simon & Schuster, 2014).
2. Gregory H. Stanton, "The Ten Stages of Genocide," Genocide
Watch, http://genocidewatch.net/genocide-2/8-stages-of-genocide.
3. Mark Fisher, *Capitalist Realism* (London: Zero Books, 2009), 16–30.
4. Nina Burrowes, *Responding to the Challenge of Rape Myths in Court.
A Guide for Prosecutors* (London: NB Research, 2013).
5. Nina Burrowes, *The Courage to Be Me: A Story of Courage, Self-
Compassion and Hope After Sexual Abuse* (London: NB Research,
2014).
6. Bessel van der Kolk, *The Body Keeps the Score: Brain, Mind, and
Body in the Healing of Trauma* (London: Penguin Books, 2015).
7. Roxane Gay, ed., *Not That Bad: Dispatches from Rape Culture* (London: Allen and Unwin, 2018).
8. Morrison Torrey, "When Will We Be Believed? Rape Myths and
the Idea of a Fair Trial in Rape Prosecutions," *UC Davis Law Review* 24, no. 4 (1991): 1013–71.
9. I've learned about this through the work of @nowhitesaviors on
Instagram. This article from them is a good starting point: No
White Saviors, "What We Can All Learn from Stacey Dooley's
'White Savior Row' & Her Refusal to Do Better," Medium, May
25, 2019, http://medium.com/@nowhitesaviors/what-we-can-
all-learn-from-stacey-dooleys-white-savior-row-her-refusal-to-do-
better-e30a2c6af0cc.
10. This empathy-limiting false belief in one's own or society's color
blindness is a powerful barrier to white people learning about the
realities of racism. It is discussed by many anti-racist activists. I
particularly learned from: Reni Eddo-Lodge, *Why I'm No Longer
Talking to White People About Race* (London: Bloomsbury, 2017),
81–4.
11. Thank you so much to Stacey for discussing this phenomenon
with me and for being so kind, supportive, and inspiring.
12. Gloria Yamato, "Something About the Subject Makes It Hard to

Name," in *Race, Class, and Gender: An Anthology*, ed. Margaret L. Andersen and Patricia Hill Collins (Belmont, CA: Wadsworth Publishing, 1995): 99–102.

13. Paulette M. Caldwell, "A Hair Piece: Perspectives on the Intersection of Race and Gender," *Duke Law Journal* 40, no. 2 (1991): 365–96.
14. Emma Dabiri, *Don't Touch My Hair* (London: Penguin Books, 2019).
15. Sofie Hagen, *Happy Fat: Taking Up Space in a World That Wants to Shrink You* (London: Fourth Estate, 2019).
16. A large part of my learning on this comes from the activism work of Munroe Bergdorf (Instagram: @MunroeBergdorf).
17. Marilyn Frye, *The Politics of Reality: Essays in Feminist Theory* (New York: Crossing Press, 1983), 1–16.
18. For a powerfully argued account of moral responsibility as it pertains to sweatshop labor and huge complex global supply chains, see: Iris Marion Young, "Responsibility and Global Justice: A Social Connection Model," *Social Philosophy and Policy* 23, no. 1 (2006): 102–30.
19. Much of my education on this topic comes from the activists of interACT: http://www.interactadvocates.org/.
20. Morgan Carpenter, "Intersex Variations, Human Rights, and the International Classification of Diseases," *Health and Human Rights* 20, no. 2 (2018): 205–14.
21. Susannah Temko, "A Different Kind of Superpower: What It Means to Be Intersex," filmed May 18, 2019, in London, TED video, 14:11, http://www.youtube.com/watch?v=Vaq4Ij0qmog.
22. David Wallace-Wells, *The Uninhabitable Earth: A Story of the Future* (London: Penguin Books, 2019), 143–57.

Chapter 7 · Exercising empathy

1. For an amazing essay on the denigration of femininity see: Julia Serano, *Whipping Girl: A Transsexual Woman on Sexism and the Scapegoating of Femininity*, 2nd ed. (Berkeley, CA: Seal Press, 2016): 319–43.
2. I think my belief in the importance of active listening, and my view that it's a skill that takes work to develop and energy to practice, owes a lot to Carl Rogers (via Kitty, of course) and the person-centred tradition in therapy he developed.
3. Hazel Carby, *The Empire Strikes Back: Race and Racism in 70s Britain* (London: Routledge, 1982): 212–35.

4. Moya Bailey & Trudy, "On Misogynoir: Citation, Erasure, and Plagiarism," *Feminist Media Studies* 18, no. 4 (2018): 762–8.

5. Trudy, "Explanation of Misogynoir," Gradient Lair, April 28, 2014, http://www.gradientlair.com/post/84107309247/define-misogynoir-anti-black-misogyny-moya-bailey-coined\.

6. Kimberlé Crenshaw, "Demarginalizing the Intersection of Race and Sex: A Black Feminist Critique of Antidiscrimination Doctrine, Feminist Theory and Antiracist Politics," *University of Chicago Legal Forum* 1989 (1989): 139–67.

7. "If Black women were free, it would mean that everyone else would have to be free since our freedom would necessitate the destruction of all the systems of oppression." From: The Combahee River Collective Statement (Albany, NY: Kitchen Table, Women of Color Press, 1986).

8. "Guilt and defensiveness are bricks in a wall against which we all flounder; they serve none of our futures." From: Audre Lorde, *The Master's Tools Will Never Dismantle the Master's House* (London: Penguin Classics, 2018), 23.

9. Particularly inspired here by Thomas Page McBee and Niobe Way's discussion of masculinity. Way suggests forgoing the question of how to be a "good man" and instead focusing on ones like "What are you doing in your life that's actually keeping the status quo?" In: Thomas Page McBee, *Amateur: A True Story About What Makes a Man* (Edinburgh, Scotland: Canongate Books, 2018).

10. Oluo, *So You Want to Talk About Race*, 53–69.

11. Jessica Valenti and Jaclyn Friedman, eds., *Believe Me: How Trusting Women Can Change the World* (Berkeley, CA: Seal Press, 2020), 1–5.

12. Roxane Gay, "Who Gets to Be Angry?" *New York Times*, June 10, 2016, http://www.nytimes.com/2016/06/12/opinion/sunday/who-gets-to-be-angry.html.

13. Sara Ahmed, *Living a Feminist Life* (Durham, NC: Duke University Press, 2017): 177–9.

14. Chanda Prescod-Weinstein, "Being Marked for Speaking Truth to Power: There's a Physical and Emotional Cost to This," Medium, October 14, 2015, http://medium.com/@chanda/being-marked-for-speaking-truth-to-power-there-s-a-physical-and-emotional-cost-to-this-398ba98e3f36.